ADVANCED
PSYCHOLOGY

Health Psychology

Mark Forshaw

Hodder & Stoughton

A MEMBER OF THE HODDER HEADLINE GROUP

1003733654

Orders: please contact Bookpoint Ltd, 130 Milton Park, Abingdon, Oxon OX14 4SB.
Telephone: (44) 01235 827720. Fax: (44) 01235 400454. Lines are open from 9.00 – 6.00,
Monday to Saturday, with a 24 hour message answering service. You can also order through our website
www.hodderheadline.co.uk.

British Library Cataloguing in Publication Data
A catalogue record for this title is available from the British Library

ISBN 0 340 859318

First Published 2003
Impression number   10 9 8 7 6 5 4 3 2 1
Year   2009 2008 2007 2006 2005 2004 2003

Typeset by Dorchester Typesetting Group Ltd, Dorchester, Dorset
Printed in Great Britain for Hodder & Stoughton Educational, a division of Hodder Headline
338 Euston Road, London NW1 3BH by J.W. Arrowsmith Ltd, Bristol.

Contents

How to use this book

This book has been designed to meet the needs of students and teachers following the GCE A2 Psychology Specification B offered by the Assessment and Qualifications Alliance (AQA). The content of this book is written to match the syllabus of the Health Psychology option topic.

Throughout the book you will find that there are various sections that have specific purposes to help you with your learning. These are as follows.

Reflective Activity   This invites you to engage in thinking about an issue and setting out your ideas and opinions before reading further.

Practical Activity   This invites you to conduct some kind of practical activity, such as a discussion among a group of friends or a mini-survey of opinions.

Study   This indicates a description of a study or experiment in health psychology. Studies have been selected that are important and/or highlight theory or key concepts in psychology. Studies or experiments are presented in the way you are required to submit them when you are asked to describe, say, a study in an examination question. When reading the study, try to identify strengths and weaknesses, and think about ways in which the study could be improved.

Evaluative Comment   This indicates critical comment and analysis. Try to elaborate on the point being made, or use the comment as a basis for small-group discussion to explore other points of view. The skills of evaluation and analysis are essential to the study of psychology and are needed if you wish to gain high grades. Evaluative comments help with the second assessment objective (AO2) examined throughout the AS and A level in Psychology.

Towards the end of each chapter you will find a number of sample questions. These have been set in the style that appears in the AQA Specification B A2 examinations. Each question shows the number of marks available for each sub-section and the marks for the relevant assessment objectives. Assessment Objective 1 (AO1) is concerned with knowledge and understanding of theory, concepts and research in psychology, and Assessment Objective 2 (AO2) is concerned with the intellectual skills of critical evaluation, analysis and application of psychology. It is important that you understand what assessment objectives are and how they are examined, since all examination questions are based on them.

Finally, at the end of each chapter, you will find suggestions for further reading. This is given in two parts: first, introductory textbooks and, second, more specialist sources. The introductory texts should be easily accessible to all students. The specialist books are more demanding and may be of value to teachers and to students who wish to try to achieve high grades or are just interested in finding out more about psychology.

I hope you enjoy reading this book and that it helps you to succeed in your studies. I also hope that it gives you a sense of how interesting and exciting modern health psychology can be.

Dr Mark Forshaw

Acknowledgements

I would like to thank Donald Pennington, the series editor, for his invitation to write this book, and for his patience and support in this adventure, and Emma Woolf for her considerable patience too. I am also grateful to my partner, Amanda Crowfoot. Never has someone in the background been so much in the forefront; ik hou van je, en ik ben blij.

The author and publishers would like to thank the following for permission to reproduce material in this book:

Figure 1.1 Cory Sorenson/CORBIS; Figure 1.2a Ulrike Preuss/Photofusion; Figure 1.2b Paul Ridsdale/Photofusion; Figure 1.3 Jon Feingarsh/CORBIS; Figure 1.5 Larry Williams/CORBIS; Figure 2.1 R.W. Jones/CORBIS; Figure 2.2 Darama/CORBIS; Figure 2.3 Duomo/CORBIS; Figure 3.2 Steve Howell/Science Photo Library; Figure 3.3 Anthony Redpath/CORBIS; Figure 3.4 Bohemian Nomad Picturemakers/CORBIS; Figure 3.5 Tim Page/CORBIS; Figure 4.1 Bill Varie/CORBIS; Figure 4.2 Maggie Murray/Photofusion; Figure 4.3 Kelly-Mooney Photography/CORBIS; Figure 4.4 Louise Gubb/CORBIS SABA; Figure 4.5 Wally McNamee/CORBIS.

Every effort has been made to obtain necessary permission with reference to copyright material. The publishers apologise if inadvertently any sources remain unacknowledged and will be glad to make the necessary arrangements at the earliest opportunity.

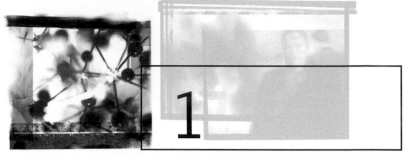

1

Health and illness

1.1 Definitions of health and illness

Consider the following examples of poor health and illness.

1. David has broken his leg and has to walk around using crutches because the plaster cast has to stay on for six weeks.

2. Amanda has caught a bad cold, which has now developed into influenza. The influenza makes her feel extremely poorly and she has only just got out of bed after five days. Amanda feels weak and shaky.

3. Emma has discovered a small lump in her left breast and following a biopsy at the hospital has been told that it is cancerous and that she will need an operation followed by chemotherapy treatment.

4. Tony has high blood pressure, which has gone undiagnosed for a number of years. The high blood pressure has caused some damage to his heart. Tony exercises regularly at the gym and feels fit and healthy.

5. Linda eats a healthy diet, does not drink much alcohol and takes regular exercise. Nevertheless, she often feels very anxious, suffers panic attacks and is often too frightened to leave her home.

Someone who looks and acts as if they are fit and healthy may not be well and could be suffering from physical or psychological illness

All five imaginary examples depict the person as ill or unwell in some way. The range of different examples provides an insight into just how difficult it is to define health and illness. For example, Tony, in scenario 4, feels fit and healthy, and is probably seen by others to be well and in 'good condition'. Nevertheless, Tony has a common illness that, if left untreated, could cause serious illness and may result in heart failure. By contrast, Emma has cancer and may fit more squarely into how we normally think of people who are ill.

REFLECTIVE Activity

Consider the cases of David, Amanda and Linda. For each, attempt to identify in what ways specifically they may be regarded as ill. Also think or speculate about ways in which each may be regarded as healthy.

You can probably think of numerous other examples of poor health and illness. What the above examples do is to demonstrate that a person may be ill in one respect but well or healthy in others. Health and illness, therefore, is not an either/or distinction that health psychologists make. Illness is not a lack of health, and being healthy does not mean a person is well in all respects – both physically and psychologically.

The illness-wellness continuum

Western societies often attempt to put words opposite to each other, as if they are genuine opposites. Some linguists call these *binary oppositions*; they are rarely accurate representations of the world. For example, what is the opposite of 'man'? You are probably thinking, 'woman'. However, the more you think about this the more you will see that this is not that meaningful. In what way is a man the opposite of a woman? Surely men and women have a great deal in common – after all, they are both versions of a human being.

REFLECTIVE Activity

Think about the differences and similarities between men and women. You may want to consider both physical and psychological similarities and differences. Make a list of all the differences and similarities you can think of. In what ways do you think men and women can be seen as opposite to each other and in what ways similar?

The opposite of 'hot' is 'cold'. However, when we call something 'hot' we do not mean that it is as hot as something can possibly be, and when we say that our soup is cold, we do not mean that its temperature is absolute zero (i.e. – 273 degrees centigrade). What we really mean is that the soup is *relatively* cold *compared* to how we would normally expect it to be. So when we are healthy or feel well, we do not mean that we are *completely* healthy, just mainly so. When we are ill, or unhealthy, we do not mean that we are totally ill or totally unhealthy, since that is likely to mean death itself. What we mean is that we are more ill than we usually are, or more unhealthy or less well than we usually are. This rejection of a binary opposition between illness and wellness (or health) leads us to understand that we have something called an

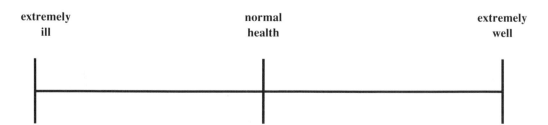

Figure 1.1: One way in which the illness-wellness continuum may be represented using a linear scale

'illness–wellness continuum'. How healthy (well) and unhealthy (ill) we are is best viewed as a point on such a continuum.

Figure 1.1 depicts one way in which the illness–wellness continuum may be depicted. Try to locate how you feel at this moment on the scale by making a mark at an appropriate point on the line. Notice that this is a subjective scale in that 'normal health' for one person may be very different from 'normal health' for another.

PRACTICAL Activity

Get a number of different people to make a mark on this scale to indicate how well or ill each is feeling at the time. Ask each person whether they suffer from any physical ailments. You might find that an older person who suffers from arthritis may indicate 'normal health' or near normal health. In contrast, a young person who has no known (to him or herself) physical ailments may indicate 'normal health' also. This exercise demonstrates that feeling well or healthy is a relative concept and will vary from one person to another.

You may have noticed that we are only a little closer to defining health. We need to go further. If we are healthy, we might say that we are well. If we are not well, we are not healthy. One way to understand this is to consider the continuum shown in Figure 1.1, but bear in mind that it is quite possible to be mainly healthy but a little unhealthy at the same time. Similarly, you can be ill, while being mainly healthy. When you have a cold, it is not particularly debilitating, but you are not completely healthy. You can still function, and you are still in reasonable health, simply less so than usual.

The second factor to consider is the baseline measurement for any given individual. What is healthy to you may not be healthy to another person. Your normal state of health can be the

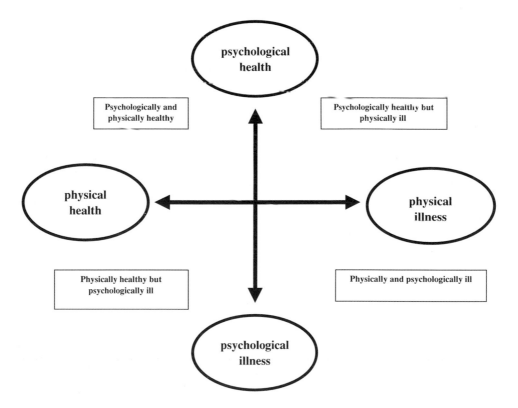

Figure 1.2: The two dimensions of physical and mental health, and the four categories created by these

baseline, even if that would be considered unhealthy for another person. For example, if you have diabetes, your body does not work properly. However, that does not mean that you should consider yourself unhealthy. Health for you is having no problems *other than* the diabetes. Therefore, a **chronic illness** such as diabetes does make you less healthy than you might be, but it is part of your normal life. Hence it can be argued that chronic conditions, such as diabetes, do not count on a day-to-day basis.

Another example is age. As we age, we become less and less healthy, or at least we can easily argue that this is the case. However, this is normal. Therefore, health for a 10-year-old is not the same as health for a 90-year-old. Individual differences are very important in the study of health, and no less so in the definition of it. We are getting closer to seeing what health is, but it is complicated, as you can see!

As psychologists, we must consider mental health even when studying physical health, since the two interact with each other. For example, having a headache makes us miserable. If we lie in bed coughing and sniffing we may get depressed. Sometimes pain upsets us, makes us cry with despair. Here we are linking the physical with the psychological. A person can be in good physical health but poor mental health, and vice versa. Figure 1.2 shows four categories related to this.

REFLECTIVE Activity

Consider each of the four categories shown in Figure 1.2 (the boxed text). Think of an example of each – for example, someone who suffers from depression may be characterised as psychologically ill and physically healthy. Someone who suffers from high blood pressure may be psychologically healthy and physically ill. Think of your own examples for each of the four categories.

We now need to consider acute and chronic threats to health. Some of what has been said above about health and illness depends upon a time factor. Illness sometimes refers to a temporary state. We are ill, then we get better. However, health tends to be something in the longer term. Therefore, it is acceptable to say that a healthy person is ill, or that an unhealthy person is well. If you do not eat a perfect balance of foodstuffs, you are overweight or underweight, and you do not exercise, a doctor would say that you are probably unhealthy. This does not mean that you are ill. In the long term, being unhealthy is bad for you, just as in the short term being ill is bad. Therefore, we might say that health is more of a *chronic* or long-term state, and illness is an *acute* or short-term thing. This is shown in Figure 1.3. Long-term unhealthiness usually does lead to illness. However, this only works to an extent. Chronic illness

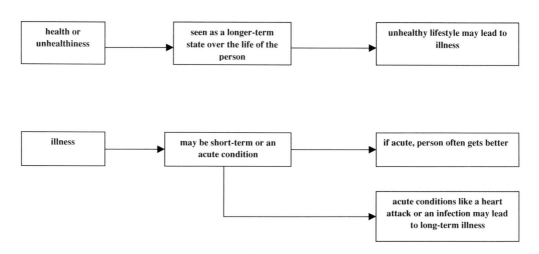

Figure 1.3: The distinction between health/unhealthiness and illness

is illness that lasts a long time, possibly for life. When this happens a chronic illness may affect our general sense of healthiness.

Now you can probably see the difficulty health psychologists face. The person on the street may use the terms differently from how a health psychologist may use them. Somewhere between the two is the best definition, but it is difficult to see how a good definition can be achieved. This is one of the reasons why we often use what are called *operational definitions* (see Pennington *et al.*, 2003: Chapter 12). Instead of stating that we know precisely what the words we are using mean, we say that we are defining them for our own purposes. An operational definition is a way of saying 'I might be wrong, and I know that it's more complicated than this, but in order to be practical and to get on with things I am defining X in the following way …'.

REFLECTIVE Activity

Think about the problems of determining health and illness from what has been said above. How might you apply these to people that you know whom you would consider unhealthy or unwell? Consider what your baseline level of health is, and reflect on how you might use your self-knowledge to compare yourself to others. It may prove useful to include both physical and psychological health.

AN OPERATIONAL DEFINITION OF HEALTH

When it comes to defining health, it is safest to take a wide definition. For the purposes of this book, health is defined as 'the state where a person functions, physically and mentally, efficiently and effectively, with relative comfort and a sense of well-being'. Psychology is the study of human thought, feeling and behaviour. *Health psychology*, therefore, may be defined as 'the study of how thoughts, feelings and behaviours stem from, interact with, or cause, physical or mental efficiency, efficacy, comfort and well-being'.

PRACTICAL Activity

In a group with three or four other students, consider the above definition of health. Identify and discuss two strengths and two weaknesses of this definition.

Changing views of health and illness

Throughout history, illness has interested people, and views have changed over the centuries. Just as we think that we are right today, people in the past had similar feelings about their views and beliefs. In the future, people may laugh at many of the ideas we hold dear now. We must also remember that different cultures around the world have different beliefs about health and illness; there is not just one, worldwide, shared view or set of beliefs.

In one form or another, health care has probably always existed. Early views of illness (going back thousands of years) informed the very first doctors, who were often semi-religious figures, and this still occurs today – for example, the 'witch doctor' in some cultures. Illness was the key issue, since historically people were rarely interested in health itself.

Porter (1997) explains that early views of illness took two forms. The first was natural causation: disease and illness were seen as deviations from the natural order. This can include anything, from the eruption of a volcano to changes in the weather or hunger. The other theme was of supernatural causation or 'punishment from God'. People who were ill were often seen as being 'punished' by their god, or tortured by Satan, devils or demons. Indeed, conditions such as epilepsy were commonly interpreted as 'possession' by a malevolent or evil force. Early 'cures' might have involved exorcism (religious removal of a demon possessing someone) in the case of supernatural causation, eating herbs or drinking an animal's blood. Again, we must be aware that these theories have not died out, and such forms of medicine are still practised. In fact, the use of natural substances – such as herbs and other concoctions – to cure people is enjoying a comeback in the form of **complementary medicines** such as acupuncture, aromatherapy, and in Chinese medicine.

These beliefs continued until quite recently in terms of human history. It was only when science began to develop (in Europe, essentially) that the nature of a doctor's work changed. Europe experienced what was called the Age of Reason, or the Enlightenment, and there was a focus on science as a driving force in the world, to change things for the better. People started to speak of 'progress', and medical technology developed rapidly. From around 1600, advances in our understanding of health and illness became rapid. William Harvey is a key figure in this, discovering the nature of the circulation of the blood in the early 1600s. These basic 'facts' about the way the body functions led to some of the important changes in the way that we set about curing people. We now know how important the blood really is in moving nutrients and oxygen around the body.

However, 'modern medicine' as we know it today blossomed only in the last 100 years. It was in this time that psychology itself was maturing, but it was quite some time before the two began to merge. In fact, the recognition of psychological factors in health and illness was something that was not formalised until the latter half of the twentieth century. Since then, health psychology has been recognised as an important discipline contributing to our understanding and treatment of illness and the promotion of health.

The nature and scope of health psychology

Health psychology is a relatively new branch of psychology, which is, in itself, a relatively new science, little older than a century. Health psychology was unheard of until the 1970s, and when it first appeared was often called medical psychology, or, when it was taught in undergraduate medical programmes, it sometimes fell under the heading of 'behavioural medicine'. In the last part of the twentieth century medical doctors became more and more aware that they could benefit from a psychological understanding of their patients. As a result, they started to turn to psychologists for insights into some of the problems that could not be solved using traditional medical techniques.

Today, health psychology is not just an area of academic study, but, depending upon the country you are in, a recognised profession. For example, the British Psychological Society (BPS) has stringent criteria for being recognised as a Chartered Health Psychologist. Professional health psychologists engage in a wide range of activities. At present, a relatively small number deal directly with clients or patients, but when they do they can be involved in helping people to change unhealthy behaviours, such as advising them on giving up smoking, changing their diet or taking exercise. Others are more research focused, sometimes creating tools to help other health professionals know more about health behaviours. For example, health psychologists are often involved in devising and researching questionnaires to identify which people are at risk from heart disease or who would most benefit from complementary therapy. Health psychologists are also involved in the training of other health psychologists by teaching and supervising students on postgraduate courses in health psychology.

Health psychology is not just of interest to psychologists, but also to anyone interested in human health and illness. Health psychologists endeavour to discover why people behave in ways that might endanger their health. They work on achieving ways in which information can be provided to promote health so that people understand it, remember it and act on it. Health psychologists do not, generally, deal with mental illness (this is largely the province of clinical psychology and psychiatry), and certainly never seek to 'cure' it directly. However, as Bennett (2000) admits, at times the demarcations between health psychology and clinical psychology are far from clear – for example, health psychologists may treat the mild anxiety that a person experiences on first being told they have cancer.

Professional bodies (such as the BPS) continue in their endeavours to promote health psychology and to establish it as a recognised complement to medical services. Some people argue that health psychology should only be the academic study of health, others that health psychologists have practical skills to offer. You will find health psychologists employed as researchers and lecturers in universities, but also as researchers and clinicians within hospitals and other health-care settings.

REFLECTIVE Activity

Clinical psychology and health psychology can seem to overlap sometimes. Some people might say that one is simply a branch of the other. If this were true, do you think that health psychology is a part of clinical psychology, or that clinical psychology is a division of health psychology?

Health psychologists study groups of people to generalise their findings to larger groups or whole populations. They look for personality types that underpin behaviours, and seek to explain things by producing models of what happens when and why, and to whom. They experiment, they observe, they interview, they survey, they test. Reading this book should give you a strong sense of what health psychologists have to offer in the study and treatment of illness and the promotion of health.

Not all health psychology need be, or indeed is, focused on groups and the behaviour of types or classes of people. Equally, it can be about individuals and their very idiosyncratic health problems. Psychologists, on the whole, have an equal interest in the nomothetic and idiographic (see Pennington *et al.* 2003: Chapter 9) approaches to the study of human behaviour. The *nomothetic* approach concerns groups, while the *idiographic* approach looks at behaviour at the level of the individual. Psychologists tend to have preferences for one approach over the other, just as they may have preferences for quantitative research over qualitative, but in health psychology itself both approaches are represented.

You will find in your reading that health psychologists often have to be quite eclectic, turning to other disciplines like sociology at times. Health psychologists cannot ignore inequalities in health, for instance. If someone lives in a culture where sugary foodstuffs (sweets) are valued, and the culture is poor, it will mean that all cannot afford to pay for their teeth to be regularly examined and repaired by a dentist. This might explain why such groups of people have poor dental health. It also might explain why they do not seem to place a great deal of value on having clean, strong teeth. Often a sociological model explains behaviour better than psychology. Health psychologists must be open to studying the full range of factors that affect a person's health status. You can expect, therefore, to read in health psychology literature (including this book) about things said by sociologists, health scientists, medical anthropologists, health lawyers and the like. Health psychologists do not ignore information from any source or discipline (as mentioned above, they take an eclectic approach) provided that it is useful to them in working out what is going on in a person's mind, which may determine how a person thinks about their body and how they treat it.

EVALUATIVE COMMENT

Eclectic approaches (see Pennington *et al.* 2003: Chapter 9) are generally more valuable than non-eclectic ones because they do not ignore anything that might be relevant. If psychologists really want to know something about human beings they must consider everything that could affect them. Individual people can be affected in significant ways by seemingly trivial events in their lives, or in the lives of others, which then impinge on their own lives. People are influenced by their upbringing, by their peers, by their financial status, by whims, by ambition, by culture, by society, by law, by random events that occur, and sometimes, seemingly, by nothing at all. When a psychologist undertakes to discover why someone does something, they take on the world in all its complexity. They need all the help they can get, and they may choose to look in all sorts of places. These might, at times, include sociology, the law, biology, medicine, anthropology, and autobiographies or works of art.

Health psychology, like the rest of psychology, should, ideally, concern itself with both top-down and bottom-up explanations of phenomena. A top-down explanation looks at everything from within a particular theoretical framework. The theory comes first. A bottom-up explanation involves developing theories from looking at the evidence first. Both are valuable in their own ways. For example, if we were trying to predict a person's chances of having a heart attack, then a top-down health psychology approach might look for evidence of a heart-disease-prone personality, based upon the theoretical premise that personality underpins most human activity. The bottom-up approach would look for behavioural aspects of heart disease such as exercise patterns, stress, diet, smoking behaviour, and so on. Of course, the health psychologist takes both a 'top-down' and a 'bottom-up' approach. A combination of what might be called *endogenous* (intrinsic or internal to the person) and *exogenous* (extrinsic or external to the person) factors will, in reality, determine if a person develops heart disease.

PRACTICAL Activity

Form a discussion group of three or four people. Each person should identify a type of ill-health or disease such as asthma, hay fever, migraine or cancer. Discuss each from both the bottom-up and top-down perspective. Talk about the value of adopting both approaches instead of simply one of them, and debate how much it is possible to consider something from two angles at the same time. Also consider from a top-down perspective the different beliefs about health and illness in traditional western cultures and other very different cultures.

In a way, health psychology is about understanding needs, and how people seek to satisfy their needs. Early work by Maslow (1962) identified a 'hierarchy of needs' that the human organism has (see Figure 1.4). Some are more basic than others, and therefore are prioritised

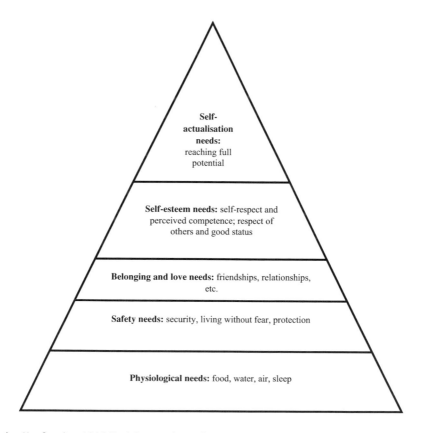

Figure 1.4: Maslow's (1962) hierarchy of needs

when the person tries to reduce their environmental stresses by satisfying their needs. Food and drink are among the basic requirements on the first rung of this ladder. Then comes the requirement for the organism to feel safe. Further up the hierarchy are more subtle human requirements such as the need to be liked by peers and to be loved. Then, above this, is the more subtle need for esteem. Satisfying all needs is necessary for the highest level of well-being possible for the individual. Unsatisfied or unmet needs cause strain or stress upon the individual.

You can probably see how closely health-related behaviours can be mapped onto this hierarchy-of-needs framework. Many health-supporting and health-injurious behaviours are underpinned by needs from this hierarchy. Health psychology is partly concerned with appetitive behaviour: people eating too little or too much, smoking, engaging in harmful sexual practices, and so on. In doing these things, they are working to satisfy needs in Maslow's hierarchy. This is probably why health psychologists will always be required – there will always be human beings spurred on by fundamental drives to perform acts that, ultimately, are damaging to them.

REFLECTIVE Activity

Consider each of the levels in Maslow's hierarchy of needs. Identify one specific need for each level and note how this may affect the health and illness of a person.

EVALUATIVE COMMENT

As psychologists learn more and more about how much of our health is psychological, we can clearly see the value of health psychology in respect to many health professions. It is not just medical doctors that benefit from the skills and knowledge of the health psychologist. Dentists, occupational therapists, nurses, physiotherapists and dieticians do too. Hence, the future for health psychology seems bright and the outlook for high-quality patient care can only improve.

1.2 Models of health and illness

Health psychology is driven largely by the **biopsychosocial model** of health and illness. It arose partly as a reaction to the older, prevailing 'biomedical' or **medical model**. As you would imagine, the medical model is largely associated with the early views of medical doctors and other health professionals such as nurses. Doctors have changed a lot in their outlook in recent years, however the medical model still prevails. It is best defined in terms of its assumptions and features.

The biomedical model

The medical or biomedical model is based on a centuries-old conception of science, and the view that there is a reality, a truth, 'out there' to be assessed and recorded. This is known as **positivism**. Positivism still drives most science today, and indeed a great deal of modern psychology is positivistic in nature. The idea is that if something really exists, it can be recorded or measured. Similarly, if something cannot be measured, it does not exist. Positivists believe in evidence. Evidence of the senses is not enough, it must be evidence gathered from scientific exploration, through careful and controlled experimentation.

Another assumption of the biomedical model is **reductionism**, or the view that, eventually, all phenomena can be explained by reduction to chemicals, cells and processes. As you would imagine, this was, and still is, the view that the medical profession tends to have. At some point in the distant future it is possible that reductionist explanations will tell us everything there is to know. It is certainly possible that *everything* might boil down to genes and their chemical actions. After all, every human being is made up of chemicals and nothing more. It might be that we can eventually track chemicals in the body and identify every possible feature of a person, including who they will fall in love with and why they like eating cabbage but hate eating parsnips. It is unlikely that we will reach this point soon, though, if ever. Scientists are engaged in furious debate about which chemicals in which combinations and proportions are responsible for which aspects of behaviour.

REFLECTIVE Activity

Think about how the assumptions of positivism and reductionism may or may not make sense in relation to health psychology. Let us take the case of psoriasis, for instance. Psoriasis is a skin disorder that causes the skin cells to be created too quickly, resulting in cracked and flaking skin. It is known to have a psychosomatic element. Positivists would aim to discover a cure for psoriasis based upon experimentation, and would agree with reductionists that the likely cure is based upon an understanding of the chemical processes that cause the skin to behave wrongly. Positivists are likely to believe that the skin is the real problem. To what extent do you think that this is where research money should be spent? Is there perhaps a reason for spending money on research into the thoughts and feelings of people with psoriasis?

One of the features of the medical model is the idea of an *expert/lay distinction*. The doctor is the expert, and the patient is not; the patient is the 'lay person'. The doctor's role is to provide advice and to achieve a cure. The patient's role is to listen and to comply with this advice. They are in the doctor's hands. However, we know that this is not the case. Patients often do not listen to their doctors or do not trust them, and will try to help themselves in ways the doctor might not have advised. Doctors need to ask questions to understand the patient, and so there is, in reality, a two-way process in action.

The medical model also has the feature of *mind–body dualism* – that is, the mind and the body are seen as separate entities to be studied and assessed as such (see Pennington *et al.*, 2003: Chapter 11). The conception of mind–body dualism is a distinct feature of the medical model, but is conspicuously lacking in eastern medical systems such as Chinese medicine. Traditional Chinese doctors are interested in the whole person, and would not make a diagnosis without learning something about the person, their likes and dislikes, habits, behaviours and personality. They believe, probably quite rightly as evidence from health psychology shows, that all aspects of a person, both physical and psychological, create the health status of an individual, not just what is happening to their body. Interestingly enough, this holistic view is a fundamental assumption of the biopsychosocial model of health and illness.

PRACTICAL Activity

In a small group, discuss the mind–body dualism problem in relation to health. How might the mind be able to affect physical and mental health? Discuss one way in which the body can affect the mind or psychological aspect of a person. Discuss one way in which the mind or psychological state of a person may affect their body.

Some academics and clinicians (e.g. Ogden, 2000) are very scathing about the medical model, but it does have its successes and strengths. These are generally in the realm of clearly physical illnesses. A broken leg can be fixed using the 'science' of medicine. Most people with a broken leg can be helped in the same way, and most of the time the treatment will be effective. The same applies to a great many other physical conditions, from removal of cysts to vaccination. However, not *all* people respond to these things in the same way, and the way that their thoughts shape their behaviour is highly relevant. There are thousands of illnesses and diseases that have a clearly identifiable psychological component. Indeed, some psychologists would argue that every health concern involves an interaction between the mind and the body. Any doctor will tell you that two patients with the same illness will not show exactly the same pattern of symptoms, and certainly will display different thoughts and feelings about their illness. An acceptance of this individualistic nature of illness is part of what the biopsychosocial model is about.

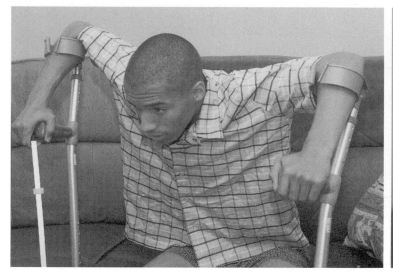

According to reductionist views of health, a broken limb is treated in the same way no matter who the patient is

EVALUATIVE COMMENT

The biopsychosocial model of health and illness is strongly influenced by the ideographic approach (see Pennington *et al.*, 2003: Chapter 11). There is an acceptance that patients are individuals. Everyone has a story to tell, and no two people are alike. If politicians and religious leaders tell us that we are all unique, all special, and all have something different to contribute, then it must also be true that these things apply when we happen to be ill. Individual differences can show themselves in a variety of ways, from whether or not a patient realises that they are ill, to their decision to go to see a doctor or to avoid doing so, right through to the way that bodies react to drugs and how people react to illness and a doctor's attempt to provide a cure.

CURRENT PERSPECTIVES

Most health psychologists accept that people are biological organisms, and that their biology can determine a lot of their behaviours, but also realise that thoughts and feelings can have a significant influence on what a person does and does not do. The medical model became increasingly outmoded as health psychologists began to generate more and more questions it could not provide answers for. A model that ignores the individual, that ignores culture, society, religion, individual differences in personality and cognition and emotion is not going to be able to answer questions like 'Why do teenagers take up smoking?' and 'How stressful is divorce?'. The biopsychosocial model is a framework for answering such questions, with its emphasis on understanding the person in the context of their life, while not losing sight of the biological underpinnings of our existence.

The biopsychosocial model

The main assumptions of the biopsychosocial model are as follows.

BIOLOGICAL UNDERPINNINGS

Within the model, there is no denial of the biological and physical aspects of health and illness. To do so would be to ignore the basic fact that we have bodies and that those bodies can malfunction just like a machine. However, physical malfunctioning is seen as a basis for

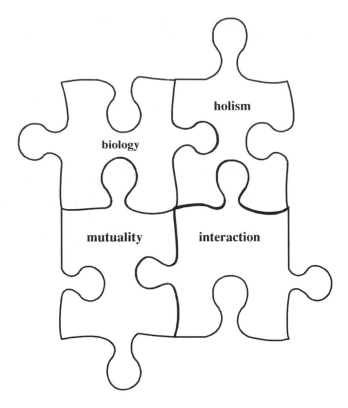

Figure 1.5: A representation of the biopsychosocial model of health and illness, showing the four main assumptions and how they slot together conceptually

understanding health problems, rather than the beginning, the middle and the end of them.

INTERACTION OF FACTORS

There is a strong recognition that many different factors interact with each other to create health and illness. Social and cultural circumstances, psychological make-up such as personality and temperament, and physical impairment, all have an impact on each other. These interactions can occur in any and all directions. A person can create stress for themselves, and once stress is created it can cause physical ailments. Those physical ailments can then cause the person to worry, creating more stress, and so on.

MUTUAL EXPERTISE

The idea of the doctor as an expert and the patient as a lay person or novice is seen as wrong in the biopsychosocial model. While it is true that the doctor may know things that the patient does not, the converse also applies. The patient owns their body. They are responsible for it, and they can tell the doctor things that help them to understand what is happening. They know about their own lives, and their thoughts and their emotional responses. Therefore, there is an emphasis on the interaction between doctor and patient. The two work together. Just as when physicists or engineers work on a tricky problem, two heads are generally better than one.

HOLISM

This is another way of describing the interaction that occurs between biological, psychological and social aspects of health, and our way of responding to health concerns. Holistic approaches concentrate on how everything fits together. The whole person is treated, rather than a particular illness.

REFLECTIVE Activity

Think of a common illness such as a cold, upset stomach or influenza. Relate each of the four assumptions of the model shown in Figure 1.5 to the illness you are considering.

EVALUATIVE COMMENT

According to Stroebe (2000), 'medical diagnosis should always consider the interaction of biological, psychological and social factors to assess health and make recommendations for treatment'. However, we should consider whether or not this is a feasible aim. Doctors are extremely busy, and by expecting them to conform to the expectations of the biopsychosocial model, we vastly increase the time spent with each patient. Depending on which source the information comes from, general practitioners have as little as four minutes on average with each patient seen. This is hardly time to get to know them, assess what type of person they are and consider their feelings about being ill. Sometimes practicalities present immovable obstacles to the implementation of our theoretical ideals.

Relationship to the biomedical model

As we have seen, there is a value to both medical and biopsychosocial models. They can work together, and it is clear that one should not replace the other. Instead, health professionals of all types should adopt a 'when in Rome' approach. Sometimes the medical model is all-important, and there is no room for the psychosocial model. When a consultant looks at an x-ray, he or she does not have to concern her/himself with the thoughts and feelings of a patient. They are looking for something very particular, very specific. However, when they have done this, they will need to talk to the patient about what has been discovered. At this point they will need communication and social skills, and they will do their job more effectively if they can respond to the patient in a way that shows understanding and compassion. If they look at all the factors influencing the life of the patient then they can create a better environment for the patient to work with medical professionals to get better.

EVALUATIVE COMMENT

Psychogenic and psychosomatic illnesses demonstrate the importance of psychological opinions on health. A *psychosomatic illness* is one that may be psychological or organic (biological, chemical or physical) in origin, but that usually involves some interaction between the physical and the mental. Almost every illness can be said to be psychosomatic. A psychogenic illness is one where there is no physical cause – that is, it is assumed to be solely psychological in origin. A good example of this is the majority of cases of erectile dysfunction (previously called impotence). If a man is able to have erections, but not when engaging in sexual activity with another person, the assumption must be that there can be no physical impairment. This, therefore, is a psychogenic problem. There is overlap between the two terms although they have subtly different meanings.

1.3 Humanistic and complementary approaches to health

It is no accident that the move towards a biopsychosocial model of health and illness has occurred at around the same time as an increase in public and professional interest in complementary medicine or in new ways of viewing health. If we are interested in all factors surrounding health, then we ought to be interested in all ways of looking at it and treating it, including unusual ones that do not fall within the everyday practice of western medicine.

Humanistic approaches

In many ways the humanistic approach in psychology (see Pennington *et al.*, 2003: Chapter 8 for a more detailed account) underlies and informs complementary approaches to health such as meditation and aromatherapy. In considering the humanistic approach to health we will look at the relevance of key concepts in humanistic psychology. The key concepts are individual experience, promoting personal growth, free will and holism.

INDIVIDUAL EXPERIENCE

Health psychology recognises that each person is unique and different, and that different people may have quite different experiences of the same illness (Ogden, 2000). For example, how different people react and behave when they have a cold may differ markedly. One person may take time off work and go to bed with a 'hot toddy'. Another person may 'soldier on' and try to continue work and domestic life as normally as possible. Individual experience within the humanistic approach in psychology recognises that perceptions and feelings are subjective, and that experience should be seen from the point of view of the individual.

PROMOTING PERSONAL GROWTH

Humanistic psychologists, such as Rogers and Maslow, regard personal growth as an essential aspect of being human. In the context of health, personal growth may be related to physical wellness, and good psychological functioning and adjustment. The former may be achieved through healthy eating and regular exercise. The latter may be achieved through the use of relaxation techniques, meditation and 'mental exercise'. Being healthy is not a static state, but something that a person may continually strive to achieve; rarely, however, will a person be healthy in each and every physical and psychological respect.

FREE WILL

Free will is a fundamental concept in the humanistic approach; it means that a person is able to choose what to do in life and to exercise conscious control over themselves and their achievements. In the context of health psychology this may be taken to mean that a person can influence and treat their own illness through complementary techniques such as meditation and visualisation. For example, Simonton and Simonton (1975) developed a visualisation technique whereby people with cancer were asked to imagine a vivid image of something attacking and destroying the cancer. One person imagined a shark chasing and eating small fish. Here the shark is the person exercising free will against the cancer (small fish).

HOLISM

In humanistic psychology a person is seen as a whole and not to be reduced to component or smaller parts such as different physical aspects and brain processes. Relating this to health psychology and humanistic approaches to treating illness, this means that the person should be treated in a holistic way. Holism is directly opposed to the biomedical model of illness since this model reduces a person to physical components (cells and cell processes) and attempts to treat a person using drugs that affect the physical components. Organismic theory (Goldstein, 1939) looks at and treats the individual holistically, combining both mind and body into a unified and organised whole. You may think that a holistic approach is more suited to psychological rather than physical illness. However, complementary approaches (see the next section of this chapter) attempt to treat both types of illness or poor health in a holistic way.

PRACTICAL Activity

Get together in a group of three or four. Each person in the group should think of an illness. Try to identify both physical and psychological illnesses. For each illness relate it to the humanistic concepts of individual experience, personal growth, free will and holism. Share with the rest of the group what each individual finds in relation to the illness he or she has chosen.

EVALUATIVE COMMENT

The humanistic approach in psychology has not been directly related to health psychology. Nevertheless, many of the key concepts and assumptions that underlie the humanistic approach inform complementary approaches to health. While, as we shall see in the next section, complementary approaches to health are often used in conjunction with biomedical approaches and treatments, the humanistic approach may be seen to be in opposition to the biomedical approach. This is because the concepts of holism, free will and recognising the importance of individual experience are usually ignored by the biomedical model of health and illness.

Complementary approaches

DEFINITIONS

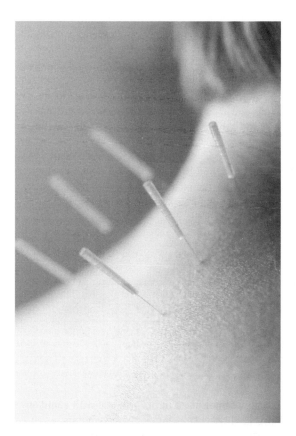

Acupuncture is one of many complementary therapies which claim to have a good success rate at reducing pain

Generally, the term 'complementary medicine' is now used instead of 'alternative medicine'. There is a good reason for this. Suggesting that something is an alternative to orthodox medicine or the biomedical model of health and illness may lead a patient with a serious illness to think that they do not have to see their doctor. This can be a very dangerous situation. The term 'complementary', however, does not have this connotation. Complementary medicine works *alongside* what doctors do – it *complements* it, it does not replace it. Today, any sensible complementary practitioner will always advise a patient to see a doctor in addition to seeking their own services.

There is a vast range of complementary approaches worldwide. Some are complicated systems of medicine that rival orthodox medicine, such as Indian (Ayurvedic) or Chinese medicine, but others are much more focused and specific, such as biofeedback, which involves learning to control bodily mechanisms such as the heart rate in order to alleviate problems such as anxiety and insomnia. We can only deal with a small selection of these approaches here to give a flavour of what exists and how they can help some people some of the time.

AROMATHERAPY

Aromatherapy is a word used to describe a range of approaches to health, including both cure and prevention. Aromatherapy is the most commonly used complementary therapy in the United Kingdom (Kuhn, 1999), and many supermarkets carry products that trade on its popularity. At the base of aromatherapy is the use of what are called 'essential oils'. These are concentrated natural substances derived from the leaves, bark, roots or other parts of plants. In some ways, aromatherapy is similar to orthodox medicine: both involve the use of chemicals. Essential oils are purported to work on both the mind and the body. They may have curative effects on the physical structures of the body, or they can have effects on the mind. For instance, lavender is claimed to have a relaxing effect, and mint is supposed to stimulate the mind, preparing someone for a session of, say, problem solving.

Essential oils can be absorbed in a variety of ways, including, quite commonly, through massage. By this means, the therapy benefits from a double effect. First, there is the effect that may come about if the essential oils can genuinely promote good health through their chemical properties. Second, massage is good for a person because it involves manipulation of the body's tissues, but also because it involves touch. When you hurt yourself, you often automatically rub the spot where the pain is. Gentle manipulation can promote healing. Furthermore, when someone you care about rubs or pats a sore area it feels good because you are on the receiving end of human care and attention. We like being touched by others, because this is a sign of goodwill or love. This is why people all over the world may kiss or shake hands when meeting or parting, or they may hug each other. Massage is an extension of this rather basic idea. Couple this with a pleasing aroma, and there is a good chance that a person will feel better on purely psychological grounds. Even if aromatherapy does not work in any other way, the psychological benefits are obvious.

As with many complementary therapies, little research has been conducted into its benefits. Of that which has, there is a split between the studies which have shown that it can work and those which show that any effects are purely 'in the mind'.

Study 1.1

AIM Diego *et al.* (1998) looked at two essential oils and their effects on a number of physical and mental processes.

METHOD They compared two groups of people given lavender oil (a relaxant) and rosemary (a stimulant), on EEG signs of sleep and alertness, feelings of depression and anxiety, relaxation, and speed and accuracy at solving mathematical problems before and after aromatherapy.

RESULTS

Odour	Alertness/ Drowsiness	Depression/ Anxiety	Relaxation	Mathematics Speed	Mathematics Accuracy
Rosemary (stimulant)	More alertness	Less anxiety	More relaxation	Faster	No difference observed
Lavender (relaxant)	More drowsiness	Less depression	More relaxation	Faster	Higher

Figure 1.6: The effects of two essential oils

As you can see from Figure 1.6, the results are mixed, and not quite in accordance with common sense. The oils seem to have had some effect, but it is strange that those people who are supposed to be stimulated and those who are relaxed are both more able to solve problems. On closer inspection, this may be explained by the fact that participants in both groups reported feeling more relaxed. Therefore, the relaxant and the stimulant appear to have had similar effects.

CONCLUSION Aromatherapy through the use of rosemary and lavender oils does have an effect on people, but not always in ways predicted by aromatherapists.

VISUALISATION

Visualisation, also known as 'guided imagery', is a technique used in a number of complementary approaches to health, and involves taking health threats (illnesses and diseases) and imagining them as physical objects and ideas. It is, essentially, a process of creating mental images and metaphors for illness. A person who has cancer, for example, may be asked to imagine the tumour as an army of evil soldiers trying to attack their body, which is a castle. The patient must, by some means, fortify the defences of the castle. In imagining such things, it is claimed that the body's natural defence systems can be 'encouraged'. To some people, this sounds a little far-fetched, almost like claims of 'mind over matter', such as when some individuals say that they can move objects with their minds. Some would argue that it is simply impossible to make the body fight a cancer just because you imagine it doing so. However, there is an increasing body of evidence to show that the mind can affect the way the body works, and the way it fights disease. The relatively new science of **psychoneuroimmunology** is the result of our researching this.

Spiegel and Moore (1997) investigated the use of visualisation with people suffering from cancer. Women were taught techniques of visualisation and followed over a ten-year period during the course of the cancer. Those who used guided imagery every day had longer survival rates than those who did not.

One way in which visualisation might work is through something called **fighting spirit**. Greer (1991), in a 15-year longitudinal study, followed 62 women after a diagnosis of breast cancer. Five reactions, or **coping** styles, were identified, including fighting spirit (see Study 2.10, page 53). The people with fighting spirit are those who accept the diagnosis but refuse to let cancer 'beat them'. They fight the illness, using all of their resources. After 15 years, almost a half of the women who were characterised by their fighting spirit were alive, compared with less than a fifth in the other coping-style groups. This seems to suggest that fighting an illness, which is largely a psychological response, does work. Without entering into details here, the research into fighting spirit, however, remains balanced; studies both for and against its protective effect exist. One thing is sure, however: fighting spirit must be related in some way to fighting metaphorically, through guided imagery.

MEDITATION

Meditation is a form of relaxation (mainly achieved mentally, although having some physical effects) associated with certain spiritual philosophies such as Buddhism. It is related to yoga, which is a kind of *physical* meditation. Within Buddhism, it is perceived as a way of cleansing the mind of the litter of daily thoughts that build up, and a means of focusing on 'nothing', as far as is possible. In the West, it has also been adopted by those seeking to find relaxation, sometimes as part of courses to train people in the workplace to reduce stress. In this sense, it is purely for relaxation, and does not have a spiritual dimension to it, as such.

During meditation, a person focuses on some tiny aspect of the environment, such as a small object they are imagining (a mandala), or the sound of their own voice humming (a mantra). They sit comfortably, and breathe slowly and deeply. Their cardiovascular system slows down. This is exactly the opposite of stress, where the heart rate and blood pressure would climb. Therefore, it is a relaxing state to find oneself in, and it is good for health. Some forms of meditation involve concentration on the object or sound, ignoring all else. Other forms involve allowing all other thoughts to wash over the individual without reacting to them in the way they normally would.

In a way, meditation can be seen as a form of waking sleep, but to some people it is a way in which we can deal with our problems by pushing them away. For other people, meditation

is a form of hypnosis, which in itself can help people to deal with their problems. Whatever the mechanism, meditation seems to have some positive effect. Walton *et al.* (1995) showed that blood pressure and stress itself could be lowered using meditation, and that doing this on a regular basis increased these effects.

Meditation can also be used in an attempt to control pain and anxiety. For example, Wolpe (1958) used relaxation and meditation techniques to help people who suffered from phobias, such as a fear of spiders, snakes or heights. A particular type of meditation called 'transcendental meditation' (TM) uses a mantra or spoken sound, such as 'om' (also written 'aum'), which is focused on during meditation. This has been shown to be beneficial in pain control.

Study 1.2

AIM French and Tupin (1974) investigated the effects of meditation and relaxation techniques on controlling and reducing pain in cases resistant to medical treatments.

METHOD A case study approach was adopted whereby individuals suffering from different types of severe and chronic pain were trained in meditation and relaxation techniques. One case was of a 22-year-old man who had a bullet wound in the abdomen and hip. This caused him severe pain over a three-month period and made him depressed, irritable, anxious and unable to sleep.

RESULTS After being trained in meditation and relaxation techniques and using these, the man was able to sleep, generally felt more positive and recovered his appetite. In all cases reported in French and Tupin's study individuals felt able to control their pain, and they felt better psychologically.

CONCLUSION Meditation and relaxation techniques may help a person control chronic and severe pain, and may result in them feeling better psychologically.

Meditation may be good for a person's health since it slows down the body's processes and helps alleviate stress

PRACTICAL Activity

Do an Internet search for sites advertising complementary therapies. Look at the ways in which practitioners talk about and advertise the therapies they provide. Do you notice any differences and similarities between their approaches and how doctors talk about health and illness?

Evaluation of complementary approaches

THE PLACEBO EFFECT

Critics of complementary therapies often claim that their success is 'all in the mind'. To some extent, this is true, but we must remember that all medicine benefits from a little imagination on the part of the patient. In the study of health and medicine there are many examples of the relationship between thoughts, feelings and actions and the way the body works. One of the clearest ways in which it can be demonstrated that the mind and the body work closely together is with respect to **placebos**. A placebo is a neutral substance, such as water or chalk pills, which can have a positive and curative effect on a patient, even though, pharmacologically, it ought not to because it is not a 'real' drug, or a 'real' therapy. Chemically, it simply does not seem to work; physically, there is no reason why it should produce changes in the body. Of course, for the people for whom it does work, it is very real, and very effective. Here we examine some ways in which health psychologists, among others, have studied placebo effects.

Most doctors accept that taking medicine is associated, to some degree, with a placebo effect. This applies to both orthodox medicine and complementary approaches, such as Chinese medicine, Ayurvedic medicine, reflexology, **homeopathy**, and so on. The word placebo literally means 'I will please', and there is much to be gained from appreciating this; being pleased is a psychological phenomenon.

For placebos to work, it is likely that certain conditions have to be met. The main factors are the attitude/motivation of the patient, the attitude/motivation of the doctor, the characteristics of the treatment, and the nature of the illness. These are summarised in Figure 1.7.

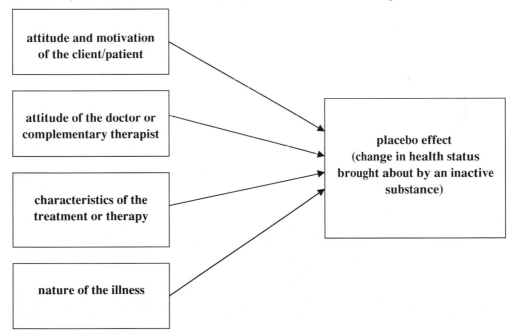

Figure 1.7: Factors influencing the presence and strength of a placebo effect

Imagine a patient with a mild illness who has faith in their doctor. The doctor believes that giving them a placebo will be helpful, and communicates this belief in the 'treatment' to the patient. The treatment is convincing enough, since it involves taking a combination of yellow and red pills at various times of day. There are even side-effects, since the doctor has given what is known as an **active placebo**, which mimics the effects of a real drug but does not have the therapeutic advantage. In this circumstance, the chance of witnessing an improvement in the patient's condition due to the placebo is high. However, let us now consider the opposite case. We have a patient with a life-threatening illness who has little confidence in their doctor and is quite opposed to taking medicines. The doctor shows poor faith in the medicine he or she is prescribing, since they describe it as 'quite experimental' and just say that 'it's worth a try'. It comes in the form of a capsule that reminds the patient of a jelly bean. Not surprisingly, placebo effects in this case are much less likely to appear. Of course, health psychology is more interested in subtle effects rather than such obvious extremes.

ATTITUDE OF THE THERAPIST

There is research to show that the attitude of the doctor or therapist is important, and that any sign to the patient that the doctor is not confident that the therapy will work is likely to reduce the patient's faith in the treatment too. As a result, not only might a placebo fail to work, but an active drug might also lose some of its therapeutic effect. As early as 1956, Feldman showed that a genuine tranquilliser lost 67 per cent of its effectiveness when a doctor presented it to a patient as something about which he or she had doubts; it became almost useless when the doctor took away its credibility. In fact, the effectiveness of a drug which can be due to placebo effects is quite often greater than the effectiveness of a real drug after faith in it has been lost by a patient.

ATTITUDE OF THE CLIENT/PATIENT

The attitude of the patient, or client, is also important in the placebo effect. Having faith in something can make a big difference to how it is perceived and interpreted. A person who believes that the laying of crystals on the body, as a form of complementary therapy, can promote healing is likely to report some change in their symptoms as a result of a session of crystal healing. This may occur partly because the person interprets any changes in the illness as being due to the crystals, but also because their belief may trigger additional work by the body's own healing systems. This latter point is something that remains to be extensively researched. So, patient attitude and motivation are key factors in the generation of a placebo effect.

Study 1.3

AIM Jensen and Karoly (1991) conducted a study to look at the different effects of patient or client expectation (belief a treatment will work) and motivation (desire to be cured).

METHOD Participants were given a mock sedative. A questionnaire was also administered to identify people with different levels of expectation and motivation.

RESULTS Both expectation and motivation were predictive of a placebo effect; however, high motivation was found to be a stronger predictor of a placebo effect than high expectation.

CONCLUSION To make use of placebo effects in helping people to get better the therapist should attempt to motivate the client to want to get better, rather than convince them that the treatment or complementary therapy is effective.

Further to the issue of patient motivation and expectation there is the question of **demand characteristics** (see Pennington *et al.* 2002: Chapter 3). This term is used by psychologists to describe the thoughts and feelings of a person who takes part in a study *about* the study itself, but is also applicable to the thoughts and feelings of a patient about the clinical consultation.

Essentially, people try to figure out psychological experiments, and their behaviour, either consciously or unconsciously, begins to match what they think we are likely to be investigating. It is as if they want to please the researchers, by 'doing the right thing'. Of course, this is all supposition, since, quite a lot of the time, they don't really know what the researchers are investigating.

There are a number of other mechanisms through which the placebo effect might work. Some or all of these explanations may be true in any given patient at any given time. First, there is the effect of conditioning. When a person is used to something happening, a special cause–effect bond is created. When a person smokes a cigarette, they feel some positive things and they learn to associate those things with smoking a cigarette, thus making the bond difficult to break. Placebo effects might be a learned response to a stimulus. In this case, the stimulus is a drug or a therapy of some sort. People have learned to expect some relief of symptoms from being given a treatment, and so they perceive some relief even when the treatment is not 'real'. Another possibility is that anxiety is lowered by the treatment, even when it is a placebo. In the case of pain, for instance, if a doctor tells a patient that he or she is being given something that will alleviate their pain, they feel relieved and less anxious. Anxious people tend to feel more pain than people who are relaxed, so pain will be perceived as less strong simply because of a reduction in general anxiety.

The placebo effect might also work through the stress–health relationship. Receiving a real or perceived treatment might, in itself, lower anxiety and stress in an individual. Stress is associated with ill-health, and better recovery is often a product of a reduction in stress levels. Placebos can be particularly effective when the illness has no discernible organic origin – that is, where the doctor cannot find anything physically wrong with a patient. In such cases, since the illness may be largely psychological, complementary approaches to treatment may be particularly effective.

Cognitive dissonance is a concept from social psychology, but it is relevant here (see Pennington, 2002: 132). This is Festinger's (1957) idea that when we make choices in life we often do so in a way that acts to reduce the dilemmas and tensions that arise. The theory of cognitive dissonance has been applied by health psychologists in attempting to explain the placebo effect, although this alone cannot explain the phenomenon in its entirety. In essence, a placebo does nothing to us in any medical or biological sense. When a person goes to a complementary therapist, a lot of time and money has been invested in the treatment approach. So, when we are given a treatment, cognitive dissonance may occur. We need to avoid feeling cheated or stupid or misled, and we must uphold our investment. We have a choice, however subconscious, of rejecting the complementary therapy and turning our back on our investment, or of creating a situation where the treatment actually does work for us. The placebo effect is just this. We choose to 'trick' ourselves into believing that the treatment really has worked, and by focusing our attention on the positive, and ignoring the negative, we get a good result.

Totman (1987) gives a good account of this experience of cognitive dissonance and how it can lead to placebo effects. According to Totman, people usually like to justify their behaviours, both to themselves and to others, and they must also feel like they have control over what they do. When a person invests in a treatment that does not seem to work, cognitive dissonance occurs because the person chose to seek and accept this treatment, but the act of doing this cannot be justified because it did not work. A reframing of the situation so that the treatment is perceived to work reduces the dissonance, and all is well.

Totman (1987) argues that this explains the placebo effects that allegedly underpin a great many complementary medicines. Non-standard health interventions are big business, and if people did not perceive them to work, at least some of the time, then they would simply give up on them. We know that many people have a great deal of faith in their favourite complementary therapy, just as many people have strong religious faith. Those people who invest in complementary medicines might be equally annoyed at Totman's suggestion that they do not work other than by convincing the person that they had better find use in them since they have paid a lot for them.

PRACTICAL Activity

Invent your own complementary therapy, and think about how it might help some people some of the time. Why might your therapy appeal to some people, and why might it not appeal to others? Make a list of your thoughts and see if you can pair them up into contrasting ideas.

Placebo effects are not always found, even when the circumstances for their occurrence may be ideal. Merikle and Skanes (1992) investigated possible placebo effects associated with subliminal self-help tapes. Subliminal self-help audiotapes rely upon a hypnosis-like effect, whereby people are given suggestions to eat less, stop smoking, and so on, below the level of conscious hearing. Very, very quietly, there is a voice on the tape, making suggestions to the listener. They cannot 'hear' them consciously, but there is some evidence that people can still take in information that they are not consciously aware of. Have you ever walked down the street and thought about someone only to see them immediately afterwards? This usually happens because you *have* already seen them, but the fact of having seen them has not entered your conscious awareness.

Study 1.4

AIM Merikle and Skanes (1992) examined the placebo effect in overweight women who firmly believed that such tapes could help them to lose weight. Thus the right conditions for an observed placebo effect were ensured.

METHOD The participants were divided into a 'real' subliminal tape group, a mock subliminal tape group and a control group who were given no tape at all. The women in the real and mock groups were not aware of which type of tape they had been given.

RESULTS Over the course of the study, all three groups lost weight, and the average weight loss was the same for all groups.

CONCLUSION As we can see, placebos cannot be assumed to be present for all remedies and cannot be assumed for the most 'gullible' or faithful people. Furthermore, the study provides some evidence to suggest that such methods of weight loss are not actually worth pursuing for most people.

It may prove helpful to summarise the factors involved in the placebo effect. Placebo effects may occur because of a combination of the following.

- Patient expectations: if the patient believes in the treatment, and wants to get better, then the conditions are right for placebo effects.

- Doctor expectations: if the doctor has a belief in the treatment, this encourages placebo effects.

- Conditioning effects: throughout people's lives they associate doctors with getting better. Therefore seeing a doctor provokes feelings of health.

- Stress and anxiety reduction: being 'treated', even falsely, reduces anxiety and stress, thus engendering the conditions for health.

- Misattributions and altered perceptions: naturally occurring changes in the illness are mistakenly attributed to the effects of the 'treatment'. People focus their attention on certain signs and away from others, which gives the impression of a cure being effected.

- Degree of credibility of the therapy: greater placebo effects are associated with treatments that are perceived as bona fide.

- Demand characteristics: people want to please their doctor, and so get better, or report getting better, in order to do so.

PRACTICAL Activity

In a group of three or four, identify a different complementary therapy for each group member to consider. Get each person to relate the seven factors involved in the placebo effect (listed above) to the complementary therapy. Once everyone in the group has done this, ask each person to summarise their analysis for the group. Look for common themes in what each participant presents to the group.

1.4 Sample questions

SAMPLE QUESTION

(a)   Explain what is meant by the illness–wellness continuum.
      (AO1 = 2, AO2 = 2)   *(4 marks)*

(b)   Outline two reasons for the emergence of health psychology.
      (AO1 = 4)   *(4 marks)*

(c)   Discuss at least two ways in which views of health and illness have changed throughout history.
      (AO1 = 4, AO2 = 8)   *(12 marks)*

      Total AO1 marks = 10 Total AO2 marks = 10 Total = 20 marks

QUESTIONS, ANSWERS AND COMMENTS

(a)   Outline two assumptions of the biopsychosocial model of health.
      (AO1 = 4)   *(4 marks)*

(b)   Outline and explain one difference between the biomedical and biopsychosocial models of health and illness.
      (AO1 = 2, AO2 = 2)   *(4 marks)*

(c)   Discuss one complementary approach to health and illness.
      (AO1 = 4, AO2 = 8)   *(12 marks)*

      Total AO1 marks = 10 Total AO2 marks = 10 Total = 20 marks

Answer to (a)

Two assumptions of the biopsychosocial model of health are that it is holistic – that is, it looks at the whole person and not just the physical side of health – and that it takes into account the cultural aspects of a person's life.

Comment: This answer correctly identifies two assumptions of the model and gives some descriptive detail of the holistic assumption. No descriptive detail is provided for the cultural assumption identified. This answer would be awarded 3 out of the 4 marks available.

Answer to (b)

One difference between the biomedical model and biopsychosocial model of health and illness is that the biomedical model is more concerned with diagnosis and treatment of illness, and the biopsychosocial model is more concerned to prevent illness and promote health. This means that the biomedical model only deals with illness after a person has got it – for example, heart disease. In contrast, the biopsychosocial model attempts to stop a person getting heart disease in the first place by getting people to eat a healthy diet and take plenty of regular, hard exercise.

Comment: A good, full answer in which the candidate identifies a more complex difference between the two models, and then goes on to discuss the consequences of the difference by each model. This answer would attract the full 4 marks available.

Answer to (c)

Aromatherapy is one complementary approach used in health psychology. Aromatherapy uses essential oils such as lavender or rosemary, and gets a person to breathe these oils through massage or a steam bath. Little objective evidence exists concerning the effectiveness of using this different approach.

Sample questions, answers and comments

However, it is more likely to be used to promote health by getting a person to relax and 'chill out'. Aromatherapy may also be useful in treating a stressed-out person since it may help with relaxation and hence get rid of stress. One advantage of aromatherapy is that even if it does not work it is quite harmless and does not have any unwanted and horrible side-effects. In contrast, treating people with cancer using chemotherapy makes people feel ill and sick, and may not always make them better.

When using aromatherapy therapy to treat an illness such as extreme stress it is often difficult to know what actually works since a person suffering stress may also be given drugs by their doctor. Hence, aromatherapy as a form of complementary medicine is often used as well as a biomedical approach such as drug treatment. Both approaches may work for the person, but how does a health psychologist find out whether or not complementary medicine has any effect at all? It may just operate as a placebo.

Comment: This answer correctly identifies aromatherapy as a type of complementary approach used in health psychology and then goes on to provide correct descriptive detail of the approach. There are 4 AO1 marks available for this and the answer here would attract 3 of these. The rest of the answer makes a good attempt at evaluation and analysis of the complementary approach, and aromatherapy in particular. The candidate identifies a difference between biomedical and complementary approaches, gives an advantage, and raises the issue of treatment effectiveness. The answer also discusses how aromatherapy may be used at the same time as a biomedical approach such as drug therapy. Of the 8 AO2 marks available this would score 5.

Overall the answer would score 9 out of the 12 marks available. This would put it at the top end of the 'good to average answers' marking band.

1.5 FURTHER READING

Introductory texts

Forshaw, M. 2002b: **Essential Health Psychology**. Chapter 2. Arnold, London

Ogden, J. 2000: **Health Psychology: A Textbook**. 2nd Ed. Chapter 1. Open University Press, Buckingham

Roberts, R., Towell, T. and Golding, J.F. 2001: **Foundations of Health Psychology**. Chapters 1 and 4. Palgrave, Hampshire

Specialist sources

Ogden, J. 2000: **Health Psychology: A Textbook**. 2nd Ed. Chapters 2, 14 and 15. Open University Press, Buckingham

Sarafino, E.P. 2002: **Health Psychology: Biopsychosocial Interactions**. 4th Ed. Chapters 1, 6 and 15. John Wiley & Sons, Chichester

2 Psychological aspects of illness

2.1 Managing illness

The patient-practitioner relationship

If a doctor were to give you a pill to take twice a day after meals, would you be certain of what you had to do? Which meals? Does breakfast count? What if the container label said that you could not take the drugs with milk or other dairy products? You might avoid taking a pill after a bowl of cereal or a cheese sandwich, but what about milk in tea or coffee? The simplest instructions can give rise to confusion. Success in the treatment of patients can be attributed to the time spent in giving appropriate information to them, and much failure can be blamed on poor communication.

It is not surprising, then, that health psychologists have focused attention on communication in medical and para-medical settings. Doctors and nurses often report problems in dealing with patients, talking to them and conveying information to them, and, conversely, patients often complain about the poor and unhelpful interactions they have had with health professionals.

Davis and Fallowfield (1994) suggest that the communication problems that occur often involve health professionals making mistakes such as:

- not introducing themselves properly

- not asking for additional information or clarification from the patient

- not allowing or encouraging patients to ask questions

- not asking about patients' feelings, instead concentrating on the medical 'facts' of the case

- not providing adequate information of a type the patient can utilise.

In a sense, these are the kinds of problem we might have predicted, since they are often the problems that can hamper any communication conducted with limited resources. Duxbury (2000) points to the sudden growth in books for health professionals about communication, and freely uses the term 'therapeutic communication'. Built in to this phrase is the implication that good communication is a key part of, and sometimes the most important part of, the treatment of a patient.

REFLECTIVE Activity

Think about the last time you saw a health professional (doctor, nurse, etc.), then consider the interaction that took place. What elements of the interaction did you think were positive and which negative, unhelpful or confusing? Do any of the negative aspects relate to the five identified by Davis and Fallowfield above?

Health psychologists take the interaction and relationship between patient and practitioner (doctor) very seriously

Professional-patient communication

Not only might a doctor explain information badly, the patient may misinterpret what is said, and may also wrongly recall what was said at a later time. A combination of these two factors may have the consequence that the intended message is quite different from the one the patient recalls. In many respects, doctors and patients live in different worlds and speak different languages. Doctors may think that patients know more than they actually do. Mazzulo *et al.* (1974) showed that a large majority of patients would take various drugs at the wrong times and in the wrong circumstances based on their (mis)understanding of the printed advice provided. Thioridazine labels suggested to patients that the drug should be taken three times a day. It was clear that some people interpreted this as meaning a 24-hour day, whereas others based this upon an interpretation of the 'day' as opposed to 'night', thus opening up a much shorter time period for the drugs to be taken in. When unambiguous labels were provided, the numbers of correct interpretations of the advice rose dramatically.

Study 2.1

AIM Hadlow and Pitts (1991) conducted a study to investigate how well patients understood frequently used health terms given to them by doctors and nurses.

METHOD Common terms describing health, the body and various states of health were communicated to patients by either doctors or nurses.

RESULTS Around two-thirds of the patients misunderstood the health terms the professionals were attempting to communicate. Additionally, about one-third of the doctors and nurses were not clear about the meaning of the various health terms themselves.

CONCLUSION The results of this study highlight the danger of poor communication for both health professionals and patients. A doctor who is unclear about the meaning of a term is not going to be able to communicate it clearly to the patient.

Empirical studies often look at both the nature of the interaction between professional and client, and the time spent in interaction. In addition, the level of client satisfaction with the encounter is a common measurement, along with some measure of how well the information

given has been understood and remembered. Here we concentrate on a selection of the factors involved and the research conducted into them. In considering these, it is essential we remember that any one of these in isolation is unlikely to be a key factor, and that a combination of factors will affect the relationship and the effectiveness of the communications that take place.

AGE

As we age, we tend to become better communicators, in the sense that our vocabularies expand. However, our memories tend to become worse. Therefore, on the simplest level, doctors communicating with older patients are generally more successful if they can deliver a message the patient can remember. A memorable message for a 20 year old may be different from a memorable message for a 70 year old. Kiernan and Isaacs (1981) studied the recall of drug dosage information for people over 65 and found that recall became more and more unreliable as the number of drugs to be taken each day increased. Furthermore, people were found to be more likely to forget to take drugs when taking numerous pills rather than just one or two.

GENDER

Doctors are more likely to view women as prone to **hypochondriasis** (being too worried about their health), and to take men's health issues more seriously than women's. When men and women present to doctors with colorectal cancer symptoms, for example, men get a final, exact diagnosis earlier than women (Marshall and Funch, 1986). Such inequalities stem from gender-biased attitudes, and such attitudes can shape the interaction between patients and doctors. Feminist writers often speak of the **medicalisation** of women, and how the traditionally male-dominated medical profession has involved itself in the ordinary aspects of women's lives (menstruation and childbirth, for instance), taking over control of such things (Oakley, 1980). In particular, Oakley noted how doctors often tended to argue with pregnant women over the expected date of birth, as if the women did not have any expertise to offer. When women asked about pain and discomfort, as they did in 12 per cent of questions, they were dealt with by mainly dismissive remarks from the doctors. This can make women less confident in their doctors (Oakley, 1980).

SOCIOECONOMIC STATUS

How much money a person has, and their social standing, can also impact upon the health care they receive, including the communication with health professionals that can occur.

Study 2.2

AIM Blair (1993) conducted a study to investigate the nature of communication between doctors and working-class or middle-class patients.

METHOD Working-class and middle-class patients were recruited for the study. All were given communications concerning different health problems or illnesses. Measures of how the patients interpreted these communications were taken.

RESULTS Working-class patients were found to be more likely to use terms associated with the body, whereas middle-class patients used terms more associated with feelings. Working-class patients favoured physical interventions (drugs and surgery), whereas middle-class patients preferred psychological interventions (counselling, psychotherapy).

CONCLUSION The different emphasis of the two groups means that working-class patients focus more on aches and pains, while middle-class patients focus more on stress and anxiety.

EVALUATIVE COMMENT

It might be that people from different socioeconomic strata actually develop different symptoms and illnesses. A person whose work is mainly manual (a working-class person who is a gardener or a road-mender, for instance) may be more likely to injure their body than their middle-class counterpart (perhaps a lawyer or lecturer). However, there may be greater *mental* stresses placed upon the person who is middle-class than on the working-class individual. There could also be an effect of education. It might be that a working-class person, who almost by definition is less likely to have the educational history a middle-class person does, is simply less aware that a doctor's role is to assist in all aspects of health, not just physical health. Equally, there may be a cultural taboo of mental illness in operation that affects working-class individuals much more than those from the middle classes. At the moment, this is merely supposition, since little research has been done that tests these hypotheses against each other.

ETHNICITY

The consideration of ethnicity as a factor influencing doctor–patient communication is much wider than the simple issue of language. It is true that doctors may vary in their command of the language they are using, especially if they are not using their native language, and the same applies to their patients. However, more subtle (but not necessarily less important) are the cultural differences and attitudes that exist.

What is said in the consultation is no more important than what is not said. McAvoy and Raza (1988) studied Anglo-Asian women's attitudes to contraception, and found that although many doctors would not offer it to them because they assumed it did not fit with their culture, a high proportion of them had used contraception and were in favour of its use. Thus, doctors must cast off their own prejudices and stereotypes about Asian women, and sensitively and appropriately offer them the full range of services available to all patients, letting the person decide for themselves if it is relevant for them. Remember, however, that we are not only dealing with non-Asian doctors potentially holding stereotypes about Asian women. Doctors from the same background as the women may also make assumptions about their lifestyle and beliefs.

CONSULTATION TIME

A clear finding is that more time spent does not mean better information transfer nor greater patient satisfaction (Korsch and Negrete, 1972). Satisfaction with the duration of consultation is moderated by the patient's experience of the nature of the consultation. If patients have been given the opportunity to express themselves and ask questions, they tend to be satisfied with the length of the consultation, even if it is short. Of course, patient satisfaction is a highly sought-after thing, and satisfied patients do tend to experience (or at least report) less pain and are easier to 'cure', as is evidenced by the fact that they spend less time in hospital.

PRACTITIONER STYLE

There is evidence to suggest that health professionals use age-inappropriate language when talking to patients. This can be perceived by patients as a patronising, condescending style. The language of health professionals is often similar to that used by adults when talking to children. As Toynbee (1977) first remarked, doctors and nurses' talk is full of 'baby-talk' terms such as 'slipping' and 'popping'. People are asked to 'pop' off their clothes and 'slip' into a hospital gown. They have 'bums' and 'tummies', and operations involve taking a 'peep' and making a 'snip'. People are asked to 'wee' rather than to urinate to produce a sample. Some argue that this kind of linguistic style represents the reduction of an adult to the status of a child. Naturally, some patients are likely to resent this. Equally, patients may have some difficulties with heavily jargonistic language too. If doctors use too many technical terms, patients are confused, naturally. If health professionals can find a balance between simplistic and technical language, patients are most likely to benefit from the consultation.

Study 2.3

AIM Savage and Armstrong (1990) conducted a study to examine the effect of three different practitioner styles on patient satisfaction.

METHOD The three practitioner, or consulting, styles of the doctors were directive, expert and sharing. Patients were recruited from a GP practice in inner London. Patients recruited were between 16 and 75 years of age, and did not have a life-threatening condition. In all, 200 patients took part in the study.

RESULTS All patients reported a high level of satisfaction immediately after consultation with their doctor. Satisfaction was greater where the doctor used a directive style; this was found to endure over time as well.

CONCLUSION Directive practitioner style was associated with higher levels of patient satisfaction than a sharing practitioner style. Some patients preferred an authoritative practitioner; this was where a formal diagnosis was offered to the patient.

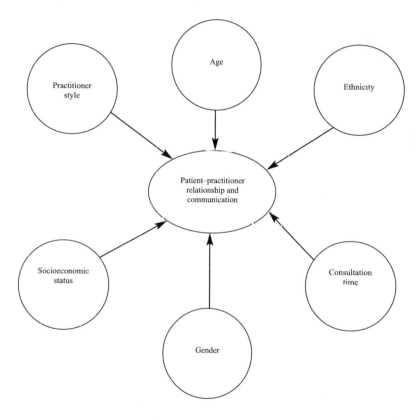

Figure 2.1: The main factors researched by health psychologists shown to have an effect on the patient-practitioner relationship and communication effectiveness

Recall of information by the patient

One of the best ways to measure success of communication with the patient is in how well the information imparted is remembered. Ley (1989) summarises this research and recommends the following to maximise the amount of information remembered by patients when it is provided to them by doctors and nurses.

- People tend to remember the things they are told first, rather than those things presented later in the conversation. This is known to psychologists as the primacy effect. Doctors can use this by putting forward the key points earlier in the consultation. Saving the best until last is unlikely to make the impression intended.

- People remember short, pithy 'sound-bites' rather than long, complicated sentences containing obscure words or jargon.

- Repeated information is better remembered, something that psychologists call 'rehearsal'.

- Specific, rather than general, information is more likely to be remembered. Therefore, talking about the patient and their particular case will be better than making more vague comments about 'people' who have 'similar' health problems to the patient.

- If the information is presented in categories that are clearly demarcated, recall is enhanced. Therefore, the information should be broken down into sections on diagnosis, treatment, self-help and prognosis. The information should be given in this order. For example, the doctor might say, 'You have hypertension. I can give you some drugs to reduce your blood pressure. You can help things along by avoiding foods with a lot of salt in them, and by losing a bit of weight. If the drugs work, and you manage these things well, you should be back to normal blood pressure within six months or so, and it ought to stay there after that.'

The above points are summarised in Figure 2.2.

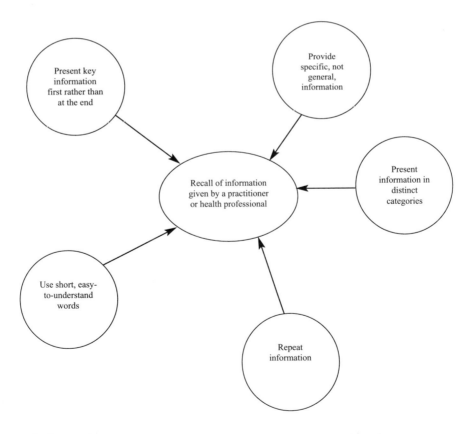

Figure 2.2: Factors found to enhance recall of information in practitioner-patient consultation (after Ley, 1989)

PRACTICAL Activity

Think of some information that a doctor or pharmacist might want to give to a patient. You could try to extract this from a leaflet found in a packet in your medicine cabinet. Make note of the dosage instructions, side-effects, and so on. Then put these into your own words, making two different kinds of instructions, one in the order given above, the other not. Read the ordered set to a group of friends and see how much they can remember afterwards. Do the same with the other set, and then see if there is a difference in the amount of information remembered.

Censorship of information

There is some evidence that doctors may censor bad news so that patients do not always receive the truth about things that are happening to them (Nichols, 1993). This may be done for two reasons. First, the doctor might be aiming to protect the patient from information they feel might harm them. Indeed, under current English law a doctor may withhold any information from a patient that, in their opinion, would harm the patient, either physically or psychologically, should it be disclosed (Montgomery, 1997). However, another reason might be because the task of giving very bad news is an unpleasant one which, sometimes, a doctor might feel unable to tackle. Censoring bad news is generally a poor way to communicate. It is often done in subtle ways by implying that a patient has more hope than they really have, or by leaving out some of the more anxiety-provoking details of the course of an illness. Ultimately, the patient is often disappointed because things turn out worse than they were led to believe, and they might then turn to viewing the health professionals involved as untrustworthy, incompetent or negligent. Honesty is usually the best policy, it seems.

Elian and Dean (1985) spoke to patients who had been diagnosed with multiple sclerosis (MS), 167 in total. They found that 18 per cent of them did not know anything about MS, 19 per cent had guessed what their diagnosis was without being told by a doctor, and 24 per cent had been told by a doctor who was not the same consultant who had made the diagnosis. Furthermore, 6 per cent of the people had found out about their MS by accident, perhaps by overhearing conversations or from a hospital cleaner. Only 27 per cent of people were told about their MS directly by their consultant without having to ask. It is clear, then, that the ideal situation where the doctor making the diagnosis clearly tells the patient about the illness does not occur in a sizeable proportion of cases. The researchers also found that 83 per cent of patients interviewed did want a direct and clear explanation from their consultant, even though only just over a quarter of them actually received this.

Communicating with children

Communicating with children is often substituted for communicating with parents, just as communicating with animals is synonymous with communicating with their owners. That this is not satisfactory is outlined by Eiser and Twamley (1999), who point out that while parents might be good at giving details of what happened to the child, they may be less accurate in describing their child's feelings about what happened. Of course, children are not animals, and are often able to express their feelings and thoughts for themselves, albeit in ways different from those of an adult.

Although children do have ideas and thoughts of their own, there is some evidence to show that their **illness cognitions** are affected by those of their parents. Children learn so much from their parents that it is hardly surprising that they pick up ideas from others about their own health status. Walker et al. (1991) demonstrated that those parents who had a chronic health problem were more likely than those who had not to have children who see a doctor because they are experiencing abdominal pain. The pain is often unexplained, suggesting that the child might be imitating the parental behaviour.

Interpreting what children say about illness and their bodies should be undertaken using knowledge of the phases through which children pass on their way to 'mature' reasoning (Bibace and Walsh, 1979). What might seem a perfectly sensible way to describe something to an adult may make no sense to a child. Since children who are ill essentially have rights to have procedures explained to them, doctors who can do so effectively are those who can speak to children in ways they will understand.

EVALUATIVE COMMENT

A key issue in understanding the anxieties of children and how their concerns may prevent good communication and, therefore, good treatment is using the idea of 'stranger fear' (see Pennington *et al.* 2003: Chapter 1). Put simply, very young babies tend not to have a concept of a stranger, but then by about seven months they are beginning to develop a feeling that there are people that they know and trust and that other people are, by default, not known and not to be trusted (Berk, 2000). Hence, children of around one to two years of age can be very hostile towards, and afraid of, others, especially adults. Some children lose this fear quite early, around four years, whereas for others it can remain until around five or six years. Most of us will have met a child who hides behind its parents when strangers are around.

Physical examinations by a doctor or nurse may prove particularly anxiety-provoking for the infant. In particular, it is not easy to explain to a small child that a person who is pulling their broken arm, or is prodding their wounded leg, is 'trying to help them'. The evidence of their senses seems to suggest otherwise.

Written communication

Providing patients with written explanations of drug regimens or treatments, or self-help techniques, has been shown by a great many studies to enhance the success of communication, both in understanding and later recall. Patient anxiety may be reduced by the appropriate use of written communication. Jackson and Lindsay (1995) made significant reductions in dental patients' anxiety prior to their consultation by giving them a leaflet which explained that the dentist would be willing to stop the procedure if they signalled to them that they did not wish it to continue, either because they were uncomfortable, worried or in pain.

On the negative side, however, the positive effects of written communication are not universal. Ley (1997) makes the assertion that up to a quarter of medical leaflets would be understood by as few as a third of the people they are given to. Newton (1995) has shown that many leaflets made available to dental patients are not understood by them. We must bear in mind that health professionals are educated and literate, and may overestimate the reading skills of people less educated and less literate.

With the increasing realisation that written communications do not always lead to greater understanding or satisfaction, alternative methods of information provision are being tried out by doctors, health educators and promoters, and, of course, by health psychologists. Video is becoming a popular medium, for example. Tattersall *et al.* (1994) looked at providing cancer patients with consultatory information either in the form of a letter or on audiotape. While both formats produced equivalent levels of recall of the information contained within them, patients preferred the audiotape, thus creating greater satisfaction. Hogbin and Fallowfield (1989) gave breast cancer patients recordings of consultations where details of the 'bad news' of a positive cancer diagnosis was being outlined. Patients reported that the tapes helped them to understand their illness, increased their confidence, and helped them tell their friends and family what was happening to them.

EVALUATIVE COMMENT

When the information being presented is very sensitive and is likely to have serious consequences for the patient, some form of back-up that the patient can listen to repeatedly is likely to be extremely useful. Telling a person that they have cancer is usually extremely distressing for them. Any information imparted during the spoken consultation *after* the diagnosis has been given is almost likely to be listened to less carefully than is necessary or desirable, simply because a distressed person cannot concentrate well. (If you are reading this book with something important on your mind at the moment, think about how easily you are distracted from the text by your worries.) Audiotapes may be seen as preferable to written communications because they present information with a more 'human' touch.

2.2 Patient compliance and non-compliance

When doctors and other health professionals give advice, or recommend a specific treatment such as taking a drug, some people do what they have been asked to do and some do not. The terms **adherence** and **compliance** refer to the act of following the advice given. Many health psychologists prefer the term adherence over compliance, because compliance implies 'giving in' to something, whereas adherence implies 'sticking to' something. Since the treatment of illness is increasingly seen as a collaboration between doctor and patient, rather than the application of a treatment by a doctor to a passive and willing patient, adherence is a more suitable term.

REFLECTIVE Activity

Consider both the terms 'compliance' and 'adherence' in relation to a person doing what a doctor or health professional is advising. Create two lists, using each term as a heading. List words that you think are most appropriate to each term. You should find that adherence generates words associated with the patient choosing to take the advice of the health professional. This may result in higher levels of taking advice than when a person feels they must comply with what is being asked of them.

There are factors in adherence behaviour that apply not only to patients but also to doctors. The behaviour of a doctor can determine adherence as much as the intentions, values or personality of the patient. The interaction between health professional and patient is often what determines adherence. However, once a diagnosis has been made and a treatment prescribed, a patient is often left on their own to determine the course of their illness. Adherence then depends upon how a person interprets their illness, their treatment and their symptoms.

Study 2.4

AIM Siegel *et al.* (1999) investigated factors that may help a person stick to a drug schedule and factors that may reduce adherence.

METHOD Participants in the study were middle-aged and older HIV-infected people. These people had been prescribed antiviral drugs to help prevent the development of AIDS. Interviews were conducted to discover factors promoting and detracting from adherence to the drug schedule.

RESULTS Symptoms of AIDS were found to trigger non-adherence to the drug schedule, this was especially so if the symptoms were seen to be side-effects of the anti-viral drugs. Also, failure of the drug to reduce or lessen symptoms was associated with non-adherence.

CONCLUSION If patients perceive a treatment, such as a drug schedule, to be having no positive effect on symptoms or causing undesirable side-effects, then non-adherence may be high.

REFLECTIVE Activity

Think about times that you have had to take medicine for an illness. How well did you comply with the requirements for taking it? Try to list three factors that could make you adhere to the medicine schedule and three factors that would reduce your adherence.

If a treatment seems to be doing nothing, or doing something negative, people stop adhering to it. This is particularly problematic for doctors, since two issues need to be considered. First, people cannot always trust their perceptions. Because a drug *seems* to be doing nothing doesn't mean that this is the case. Just because a person develops an unpleasant symptom after taking a drug doesn't mean that the drug is responsible for it. Second, drugs can sometimes take a while to start working. People often expect immediate or quick effects, and many drugs do not work in this way. People also mistakenly believe that when a problem *appears* to have cleared up, then it has gone for good. It is common for people taking antibiotics to stop when the symptoms have gone away, or for people using anti-fungal creams for foot infections, like *tinea pedis*, to do the same. Of course, what happens is that the remaining bacteria or fungi responsible for the problem are given a respite, and they recover and start to attack the body again. Much of what happens to the body is not visible. Symptoms are often the last stage in a long process. Careful education of patients as to exactly what to expect from a treatment can improve adherence.

EVALUATIVE COMMENT

A lot of research on communication in a health-care context remains to be conducted if we are to learn enough to make the relationships between doctors and patients effective and efficient. One individual difference that can influence the success of communication is dyslexia. Large numbers of people are dyslexic, and as yet very little, if any, published material exists on whether dyslexia can affect communication with doctors (Forshaw, 2002a). Are dyslexic people more likely to confuse one pill for another or take wrong numbers of pills? Might they forget what the doctors have told them, since memory problems are associated with dyslexia?

2.3 Pain

The mind and body are not separate things (for the mind–body debate in psychology, see Pennington *et al.* 2003: Chapter 10). One of the clearest ways in which it can be demonstrated that the mind and the body work closely together is with respect to the experience of pain. Most days, most of us experience some pain, however slight. We might even have occasionally done something to 'take our mind off the pain'. We even speak of mental pain, although the sensation of mental pain, is, of course, a different one from bodily pain.

Pain is a word we all use, and a feeling most people understand. However, if you take two people and ask them to describe a pain that you have controlled so that the sensation should be as similar as it is possible to make it, they will give you different accounts of it. There will be similarities, but there will also be differences. They may agree or disagree on whether or not it is a stabbing pain, or an ache, or whether it is a

This person looks like they are in pain, but it is not easy to tell what kind of pain they are suffering from hot or a cold pain, or on how long it persists. This is the fascinating aspect of pain, and also what makes it so difficult to study properly.

Pain is a significant factor in the decisions health professionals have to make about a person's quality of life. Is the person who cries the most the one experiencing the most pain? Not necessarily: it all depends upon the person. The first published acknowledgement that pain has a strong psychological component comes from Beecher (1946; 1956) who looked at requests for pain relief (**analgesia**) among soldiers and compared these to the requests made by civilians with similar injuries. Most of the soldiers claimed not to perceive any pain and only a quarter of them requested pain relief. In the case of civilians, over 80 per cent asked for pain relief. Beecher argued that the context in which the pain was experienced had an impact on the way in which it was perceived.

Theories of pain perception

Early pain theories focused on the physical or physiological aspects, trying to understand what was happening at the level of tissue damage. This approach was doomed because it has always been known that pain has a substantial psychological component. Some people can stub their toe and just say 'ouch', whereas others will need to sit down for ten minutes, rubbing the toe, and will continue to experience pain for hours to come. Furthermore, a person who normally tolerates pain quite well will, on occasion, be more susceptible to it – for instance, when they are very busy or very stressed. A person who is normally pain-intolerant may become quite tolerant when they are excited and happy. There is clearly a mixture of psychological and physical components to every pain.

The most enduring and famous theory of pain perception is the **gate-control theory**,

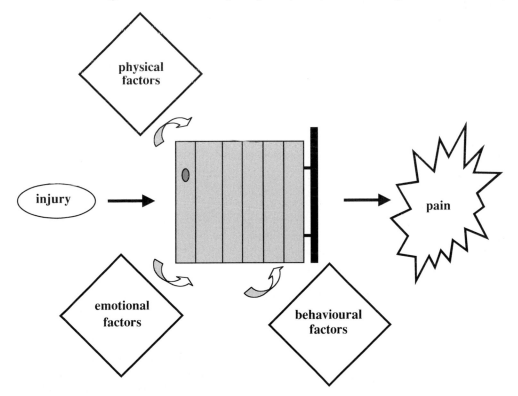

Figure 2.3: The gate-control theory of pain (after Melzack and Wall, 1965)

espoused by Melzack and Wall (1965). According to this theory, there is a barrier at the level of the spinal cord, which acts as a gateway for incoming and outgoing signals associated with the sensation of pain. When the gate is fully open, pain is perceived at its strongest and when the gate is closed there is no pain. Of course, most pain signals are being transmitted via a partially open/closed gate. The gate is opened and closed by a combination of physical, emotional and behavioural factors. Almost all pains are made up of psychological and somatic components.

The gate can be opened by physical factors such as bodily injury; emotional factors such as state of mind, anxiety and depression; or behavioural factors, such as attending to an injury and concentrating on the pain. Similarly, it can be closed by physical factors such as analgesic remedies, emotional factors such as being in a 'good' mood, and behavioural factors like concentrating on things other than the injury.

According to Melzack and Wall (1982), there are three dimensions that contribute to our experience of pain. These are *sensory-discriminative*, *affective-motivational* and *cognitive-evaluative*. The first of these refers to information about the location of a pain, its intensity, and its pattern over time. The affective-motivational dimension concerns our motivation to act on the pain, and the cognitive-evaluative facet is where our experiences of past pain may shape our perception of current pain. In combination, these dimensions of pain shape the overall pain experience. This is summarised in Figure 2.4.

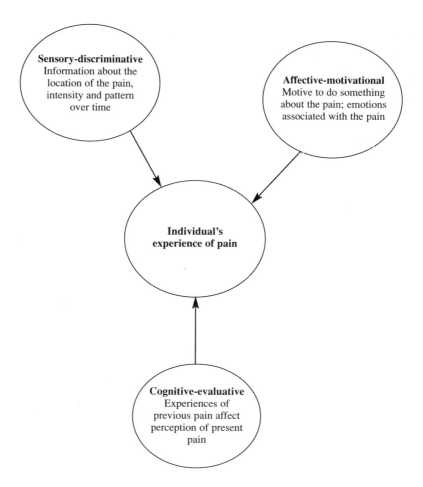

Figure 2.4: Three psychological dimensions contributing to the experience of pain (after Melzack and Wall, 1982)

EVALUATIVE COMMENT

Gate-control theory would, theoretically, suggest that there is a limit to physical pain that can be experienced. After all, an open gate cannot be 'more' open. Of course, this cannot be tested, but the fact that some people in intense pain lose consciousness might suggest that the gate has been opened fully, and losing consciousness could be a protective mechanism to prevent some kind of 'overload' to the system.

While gate-control theory represents a step forward in accepting the various contributory factors in pain perception, a problem with the theory is that it is difficult to quantify the effects of the individual factors. Just as pain itself is difficult to assess and attach a value to, so we run up against difficulties when we try to work out which factors are more important than the others, and so on. In psychology, we tend to favour models and theories that allow us to make predictions.

Gender and pain

There is some evidence to show that men and women differ in their reactions to pain. In cold-pressor stimulation tests (see page 42), women show lower tolerances of pain than men. However, women can tolerate considerable pain in certain circumstances, such as during childbirth or with painful menstrual periods. Women typically report more pain than men, and are more likely to report pain that is difficult for doctors to ascribe to a particular cause. It is, however, difficult to separate out social norms for pain from genuine differences in biological functioning. In most societies where psychological research is conducted, men are expected to be 'tough' and to accept pain. As a result, men may feel pain but are less likely to report it to a doctor.

Men and women appear to differ in their tolerance of pain, but this does not apply in all cases. Both male and female athletes tolerate huge amounts of pain

Measuring pain

Health psychologists have used three basic approaches to measuring pain; these are as follows.

- *Physiological:* these are about measuring the body's reactions to pain, such as increased sweating or heart rate, and sometimes by measuring the electrical activity of the brain. These are not often used except in studies specifically interested in the physiology, rather than the psychology, of pain.

- *Behavioural:* these measures involve the reactions of the person towards pain. When you are in pain you wince, or cry out, and if you have a sore foot you walk gingerly. Again, such measures are not often used, although they are seemingly objective.

- *Self-report:* the majority of measures used within health psychology are self-report measures.

These involve the patient responding to a series of questions about the pain. They are important because if a person claims to feel pain it can be rather cruel not to take this seriously. As psychologists, we are interested in working under a primarily psychosocial model of health, which involves listening to people and believing what they say. Of course, sometimes people do say they are in pain when they are not, either to gain attention or for some other reason, such as to take time off work. We cannot always be sure that a person is telling the truth, and so behavioural measures are also useful in corroborating a person's claims.

PRACTICAL Activity

Discuss within a small group the advantages and disadvantages of each of the three measures of pain (described above) used by health psychologists. Is one method more objective and likely to produce reliable measures of pain over other methods? Specifically, what disadvantages and drawbacks do you see with physiological and behavioural measures?

VISUAL ANALOGUE SCALE

A commonly employed and basic self-report measurement of pain can be achieved through the use of what is called a **visual analogue scale** (VAS). Here people are asked to rate the intensity of their pain by making a mark along a line that represents a scale from 'no pain' to 'unbearable pain', or something similar. By measuring the distance along the line the person has made the mark, we can get an index of how much pain they are feeling.

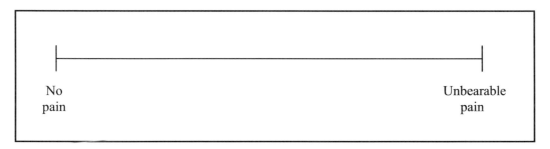

Figure 2.5: A visual analogue scale (VAS) that may be used to get a simple measure of pain; a person in pain could be asked to make a mark on the horizontal scale indicating the intensity of the pain they are feeling

EVALUATIVE COMMENT

A problem with the VAS is that only the intensity of the pain can be recorded in this way, not the quality of it – for example, whether it is burning or piercing or throbbing. It is also not a method of measurement that works well when trying to compare different individuals in an attempt to find out who is experiencing the greater pain. Quite simply, there is no way of equating the pain experiences of two people. The best use for a VAS is when comparing an individual's pain with their pain at another point in time. Since we can expect some consistency and reliability in responding based upon a person's character or general resting level of behaviour, we can assume that mostly a rise or fall in reported pain on a VAS does relate to a true rise or fall in perceived pain. Since using VAS instruments does not give information about the *type* of pain being experienced, more sophisticated tools are usually needed.

MCGILL PAIN QUESTIONNAIRE

Possibly the most well-used pain-perception measurement tool is the McGill Pain Questionnaire (MPQ) (Melzack, 1975). The MPQ is an instrument which recognises that there are four dimensions to pain. These are 'location', 'feeling', 'over time' and 'strength of pain'. Pain is not just about intensity, but about type. Thus we have hot and cold pains, dull and sharp pains, and so on. Earlier we noted that gate-control theory suggests that pain consists of three dimensions: sensory-discriminative, affective-motivational and cognitive-evaluative. These three are reflected in the construction of the MPQ. People are asked to rate the intensity of the pain (a quantitative index), along with the type of pain experienced (a qualitative index). A person is asked to choose from a list the words that best describe their pain, and then give a rating of the intensity of that feeling by numbering each word selected. For example, a person can choose between 'sickening' and 'suffocating' to describe their pain (but may not choose both), or may deselect both terms. Of course, those people who would like to describe their pain as both sickening and suffocating in equal amounts will not be well served by the MPQ. Figure 2.6 provides some examples of items from the MPQ.

1. What does your pain feel like?			
(a) Pulsing	Shooting	Stabbing	Sharp
(b) Crushing	Wrenching	Burning	Stinging
(c) Dull	Tender	Tiring	Sickening
(d) Terrifying	Gruelling	Blinding	Annoying
(e) Piercing	Squeezing	Freezing	Agonising

2. How does your pain change with time?		
Constant	Intermittent	Transient/brief

3. How strong is your pain?				
Mild	Discomforting	Distressing	Horrible	Excruciating
1	2	3	4	5

Figure 2.6: Some examples from the McGill Pain Questionnaire (MPQ) (Melzack, 1975)

EVALUATIVE COMMENT

Another problem with the MPQ is that it is not always possible for a patient to liken their pain to one of the descriptions given. Because there is such a wide variation in perception, some patients would prefer to use their own words to accurately describe what they are experiencing. Sometimes patients simply do not know what some of the words mean. Do you know what 'lancinating' means? If you are fortunate enough to do so, ask a few people around you. You will find that a large majority do not. This word appears in the MPQ. Similarly, not all people use words in exactly the same way. How can we be sure that a 'smarting' pain to one person is the same as a smarting pain to another? What smarts to one person may sting to someone else. Furthermore, the words 'taut' and 'tight' appear in separate categories in the MPQ. To many people, these words may seem synonymous. Of course, this is not to say that the MPQ is not an excellent questionnaire. Quite simply, given the nature of the phenomenon, all other instruments to measure pain are likely to be equally flawed, if not more so. Measuring the idiosyncratic or personal is always a problem for psychology, and the fact that we will never do it perfectly is not a reason for giving up.

PRACTICAL Activity

In a group, write down some of the words you would use to describe pain. Then compare lists, and think about which types of pain you have experienced. When you have done this, take pairs of words, such as 'burning' and 'aching'. Then see if you can agree on which is the worst. You will probably find that you cannot reach agreement.

BEHAVIOURAL MEASURE OF PAIN

While self-report is probably the best way to assess pain, it is not the only way, and occasionally some measure of pain based on a person's behaviour is used. This is especially valuable when faced with patients who are likely to lie about their pain, either neurotically, or exaggerating their pain to gain attention or some other benefit, or making light of it either because of denial, or not wanting to bother others. In these cases, there can be a discrepancy between self-report measures and a behavioural index. The most commonly used behavioural measure is that of *cold-pressor stimulation*. This is a measure of tolerance to pain. You will probably know that if you put your hand into cold water for a while, pain results. Cold-pressor stimulation is a controlled version of this. A person places their forearm in room-temperature water for one minute, then they put their arm in a special apparatus in water at 2°C. They must hold down a platform, under the water, until they can no longer stand the pain. At this point, reducing pressure on the platform will allow it to spring back upwards, taking the arm out of the water. The value of such a method is that people are being asked to tolerate the pain for as long as possible, and the experimenter can be sure that pain is actually being experienced. However, the social-psychological issues still pertain. Just because a person has said they cannot tolerate the pain any more does not mean that they have genuinely reached their threshold of tolerance; they may have reasons why they would like to appear more intolerant than they really are. This is something that may affect studies of pain and gender across many cultures. While women seem to be less tolerant of pain in general than are men (Goolkasian, 1985), this might be an effect exacerbated by a social pressure on women to appear 'weaker' and more 'dainty' or 'ladylike' than men. Where such social pressures exist, women may be less likely to push themselves to tolerate pain. The converse applies to men, of course, in such cultures.

PHYSIOLOGICAL MEASURES OF PAIN

The electromyograph (EMG) has often been used to measure pain. The EMG measures the electrical activity in muscles, which in turn gives some idea of muscle tension. Muscle tension is associated with pain, particularly headaches and pain in the lower back. Blanchard and Andrasik (1985) have demonstrated different patterns of EMG in a person when experiencing and not experiencing a headache. However, claims have been made that EMG measures do not provide a sufficiently reliable measure of pain (Chapman *et al.*, 1985).

Study 2.5

AIM Dowling (1983) attempted to measure pain through the physiological measures of heart rate and skin conductance.

METHOD Using the cold-pressor apparatus, measurements of heart rate and skin conductance were taken before, during and after the cold-pressor procedure.

RESULTS Heart rate and skin conductance showed enhanced activity when the arms of participants were submerged in cold water at 2°C.

CONCLUSION When there are objective ways of knowing that a person is expressing pain, physiological measures such as heart rate and skin conductance may be of value.

Managing pain

A serious issue for health psychologists is in working out ways in which people can manage their pain, especially people with chronic pain. There are many medical methods for dealing with pain, such as surgery and drug treatments, but equally important are psychological interventions aimed at enhancing a person's ability to cope with pain. These are especially important in those situations where the pain is not well managed by traditional doctors' methods.

Pain management can take a number of forms, and these can be classified as *biomedical, behavioural* or *cognitive*. Sometimes pain management involves a combination of these.

BIOMEDICAL PAIN MANAGEMENT

Biomedical interventions are the easiest to describe, but of least interest to health psychologists. These include analgesia (numbing pain using drugs such as aspirin or, in more extreme cases, morphine), and surgery to remove the source of the pain or correct an injury. Behavioural approaches tend to involve getting the person to change their behaviour either to stop them doing something that causes pain, or to adapt to the pain that they feel.

COGNITIVE APPROACHES TO PAIN MANAGEMENT

Distraction is one psychological (and cognitive) method. By shifting attention away from the pain, people can actually feel less of it. Some dentists attach a teddy bear to their clinical lamp, so that children will pay attention to the bear and ignore the treatment. Have you noticed that some people swear and shout when they hurt themselves? Again, this could be nature's way of introducing a distraction. However, distraction may not always work. While it is good for weaker pains, intense pain is not always best dealt with by distraction. Sometimes pain is so strong that a person needs to concentrate or focus on it in order to manage it. If you have ever experienced intense pain, you will probably know what it means to be unable to think of anything else.

Pain redefinition involves giving the pain experienced a new meaning. Thoughts about the pain that are negative are replaced by more constructive and positive ones. People might be taught to think that the pain is not as bad as it is, or taught to have faith in their ability to cope with the pain. In one sense, the first of these is a form of denial, which as we have seen elsewhere, can be a good strategy for certain people with some illnesses some of the time. Saying to yourself 'It's not really that painful' when it is actually very painful is a lie, but people can believe their own lies. If such lies can be therapeutic, then it makes sense to take advantage of them.

Imagery techniques to reduce pain essentially involve thinking about something else to take the mind off the pain. Thoughts about pleasant experiences like holidays, birthdays and favourite meals can be conjured up, and the pain weakens as a result. Of course, not all people have visual imagery that is strong enough to support this technique (and some have none at all). For those who have, it can be effective. It makes sense to view this as a form of distraction, at least in some ways. By thinking of something else, people are distracted from the pain.

Hypnosis is another technique, relying upon psychological phenomena, commonly used to treat pain. A number of dental surgeons now use hypnosis as an alternative to anaesthesia, with considerable success. However, hypnosis does not work for everyone. Hypnotherapists tell us that there is no point trying to hypnotise a person who does not have faith in the phenomenon of the hypnotic state, or who does not want to be hypnotised. Those who are most susceptible are likely to benefit most (Barber, 1982). Hypnosis represents a wholly psychological therapy with distinct uses in medical settings and in enabling individuals to control their own health. In the dental arena, hypnosis has two main uses. It can be applied in cases of worried patients, to reduce their anxiety (anxiety can actually reduce the effectiveness of surgical anaesthetics). It can also be used as an alternative to anaesthesia for patients who are allergic to it or have some other objection. Since, in Britain at least, general anaesthetic has been ruled out in most dentists' practices because of the danger to life associated with it, hypnosis is beginning to present a feasible alternative for some patients.

BEHAVIOURAL PAIN MANAGEMENT

Operant conditioning (see Pennington *et al.*, 2003: Chapter 5) is a behavioural technique that has been employed in pain management. Operant conditioning techniques involving the use of reward and punishment are employed to change a person's behaviour. Often, nurses, parents and friends inadvertently reward someone for complaining of pain or crying because of a pain. They are rewarded because the person is being paid attention by others. To stop a person focusing on their pain the operant conditioning approach to pain management does not reward such behaviours – they may be ignored or even punished – to achieve extinction of the behaviours. Health psychologists may use the principles of operant conditioning as follows:

- by ignoring pain-related behaviours shown by a person

- by rewarding behaviours that focus on things other than the pain.

EVALUATIVE COMMENT

Studies assessing the value of operant conditioning for pain management have produced mixed views. For example, Turk *et al.* (1992) have shown that operant conditioning can result in people taking less medication. Here it is assumed that taking less medication means that the pain is being better managed and not on the person's mind all of the time. However, not all pain has been found to benefit from this approach – it seems that enduring or chronic pain is less well managed using techniques of operant conditioning.

2.4 Psychological factors in illness

Psychological factors and physical health

Health psychologists have produced substantial evidence to demonstrate that many physical disorders, particularly chronic illnesses such as diabetes, asthma, migraine headaches and hypertension (high blood pressure) have a *psychosomatic* basis (Sarafino, 2002). Health psychologists do not really use the term 'psychosomatic' but prefer instead either 'psychological' or 'psychosocial'. These terms reflect the idea that to understand physical illness and poor health, psychological factors must be taken into account. Psychological factors may explain the cause of the disorder and help with effective treatment of the illness. Here we look at two common illnesses: diabetes and asthma.

Diabetes

An example of chronic illness that is common is diabetes. The hormone insulin, secreted by the pancreas, controls the levels of glucose (a sugar) present in the blood. When this system goes wrong, diabetes results. Too much sugar in the blood is called hyperglycaemia, and this leads to *diabetes mellitus*. There are two main forms of this: insulin-dependent and non-insulin-dependent, also called **Type I diabetes** and **Type II diabetes** respectively. The former is much rarer than the latter, making up no more than one-tenth of diabetes cases. In insulin-dependent *diabetes mellitus*, people must inject themselves with insulin in order to maintain their blood sugar levels, usually because the insulin-producing cells in the pancreas are physically or chemically damaged and unable to function. This type tends to develop early in life. In Type II diabetes injections are not necessary because the cells in the pancreas can still produce insulin and so regulation of blood sugar is achieved by giving nature a 'helping hand'. Quite simply, by careful regulation of diet and taking of medication the problem can be kept under control. This type of diabetes is most likely to develop at middle age, although it can occur at any age.

Diabetes is not just a health problem in itself, but is accompanied by a set of risk factors for other life-threatening conditions, and can have effects on the life of an individual over and above the challenges faced by daily injections or by being careful about food. People with diabetes are more likely to fall prey to strokes and/or heart attacks, develop kidney disease, become blind and, in men, develop erectile dysfunction. Diabetes is also a secondary complication in a number of other conditions, such as cystic fibrosis and liver cirrhosis. It is one of the most common diseases, affecting 30 million people worldwide (Gale and Anderson, 1998).

The ordinary lives of people coping with diabetes were described by the sociologist Kelleher (1988). In interviews with 30 diabetics from London, he identified three life strategies. The 'true' copers were those who fitted diabetes into their lives without changing their lifestyle significantly, and followed doctors' advice. These people (20 per cent of the sample) showed a high degree of personal control, something deemed very important by health psychologists studying chronic illness. They were in charge of their illness, rather than it being in charge of them. A total of 30 per cent of the interviewees showed what Kelleher calls an 'adaptive strategy'. These people make changes to their lifestyle, but lack the degree of control of the copers. They normalised their diabetes, accepting it as part of their lives. Their lives changed more as a result of coping with diabetes than the true copers. Finally, the most important group in some sense was the 'worriers', who comprised half of the sample. These people dealt with their illness by worrying about it continually. They tended not to be able to see diabetes as a part of their normal life, and generally rated themselves as unhealthy people, diabetes being something, to them, that made them unhealthy. Depression and anxiety characterised these people.

An important distinction between the first two groups and the last is that the latter would see themselves as primarily a diabetic, rather than as a person with social roles and a place in the world. The others saw their diabetes as secondary, rather than primary. This is the difference between what we might call a diabetic man, and a man with diabetes, or a diabetic woman with two children or a mother of two who has diabetes. By identifying this core perception, health psychologists ought to be able to work with a person to find the most suitable path through the course of the illness.

Unlike some other chronic illnesses, which may rely mainly upon management of the condition by doctors using drugs and equipment, the progress of diabetes depends on a great deal of self-management. Not everyone is equipped naturally with the skills to be able to do this. Just as there are people with tidy offices and untidy offices, or people who make good use of their time and people who 'waste' it, so there are people who are able to take control over their lives to make the changes necessary to keep diabetes in check, and there are those who find the changes in diet and lifestyle tremendously stressful. Getting people to stick to a controlled lifestyle is often very difficult, especially among certain groups, such as diabetic adolescents, who often feel that diabetes is preventing them from being just like their friends and taking part in everything they do. Furthermore, many of the dangers inherent in failing to follow self-care and self-treatment regimes (controlling diet, and so on) are not immediate ones. This means that people are not scared by failing to look after themselves in an ideal fashion because they may not notice any physical changes whatsoever – some of the problems of mismanaged diabetes will not occur for decades. The threat of a problem occurring in 30 years' time is not a strong one for most people.

REFLECTIVE Activity

Think about the last time you were ill with a cold, upset stomach or dose of 'flu'. How well did you manage to control your illness by eating the right kind of foods, taking medicine as required, and not going out or back to college too early? Most people show a degree of control but it is not usually total.

Insulin-dependent diabetics have to make calculations to determine how much insulin to inject. This is because there are a number of factors that affect how much is needed, such as exercise and stress. Therefore, rather than a set dosage, insulin requirements have to be tested using a sample of blood. If a person makes the wrong dosage choice, the result could be fatal, especially if the individual repeatedly misinjects themselves over a sustained period.

It is often said that knowledge is power. Of course, power is also about control. Can knowledge affect control? It appears so, but not necessarily linearly.

Study 2.6

AIM Hamburg and Inoff (1982) investigated diabetic children to find out how knowledge about their illness affected the control they had over the illness.

METHOD Children attending a summer camp and who suffered from diabetes were divided into three groups. Group 1 knew little about their illness, Group 2 knew a fair amount, and Group 3 had considerable knowledge. Measures of adherence to doctors' advice on treatment were taken of children in each group.

RESULTS Group 1 showed poor adherence compared to Group 2. However, the lowest rates of adherence were found in children who knew most about their condition (Group 3).

CONCLUSION Hamburg and Inoff concluded that high levels of knowledge about their condition resulted in children feeling debilitated and mildly depressed. In consequence they felt unable to control their condition. Too much knowledge may bring a sense of 'disempowerment' to the individual.

Langewitz *et al.* (1997) report an educational and problem-solving programme intended to improve self-management in diabetic people. The participants were involved in both experiential learning about the effects of various factors upon blood glucose levels and also worked through 'solutions' to problems about dosages. The programme significantly improved blood glucose levels, and reduced diabetes-related illness, showing that self-management is a skill that can be developed substantially.

EVALUATIVE COMMENT

As with other chronic illnesses, the stress that diabetes can engender in an individual must be appropriately managed in order to prevent it creating additional health problems. Since diabetes is associated with poorer cardiovascular health than the norm, stress can exacerbate this because stress itself, as we have seen elsewhere, is also a factor in heart disease. However, there is by no means a simple relationship between stress reduction and health in diabetic patients. Aikens *et al.* (1997) compared non-insulin-dependent diabetics assigned to either a stress-reducing muscle-relaxation and imagery programme or to standard medical treatment. Blood glucose levels were tested before and after the programme, and 16 weeks after the intervention. They found that blood glucose levels could actually be lowered by the muscle-relaxation programme, but mainly in the group of people who were less stressed to begin with. This suggests that – as with virtually any treatment programme, medical or otherwise – there will be individual differences in the reaction to it and its effectiveness.

Asthma

Asthma is a chronic illness that involves a malfunction of the airways. It involves bouts of difficulty in breathing, and can be very dangerous for the individual. It is a relatively common illness, and increasingly so in children, which some people suggest may be due to the large number of environmental pollutants present in the air, such as the noxious fumes released by motor vehicles, and the chemicals factories produce from their chimneys. It can be made worse by physical exertion, and can be brought on by stress.

Asthma is a particularly interesting disease for psychologists because there is evidence that it involves a strong interaction between the mind and the body. If a person has difficulty breathing, this is likely to frighten and worry them, since breathing is, of course, essential for life. Therefore, during a bout of asthma a person can develop some very distressing thoughts, perhaps that they are going to die (something we call *catastrophic cognitions*). This creates stress, and the stress can then make the asthma 'attack' even worse. Not only can a bout of asthma be brought on by anxiety, but the psychological component in this illness was clearly demonstrated by a number of studies including Butler and Steptoe (1986), who gave asthmatic participants a harmless (placebo) solution to inhale. Some were told that this was an irritant, and they developed symptoms of asthma accordingly, whereas those who were not told this did not. Furthermore, if people were given a pretend asthma drug, followed by the pretend irritant, there were fewer symptoms of asthma recorded.

Study 2.7

AIM Lewis *et al.* (1984) evaluated the effectiveness of an educational package to help children manage their asthma.

METHOD Eight- to 12-year-old children were divided into two groups. The control group (Group 1) received four hours of lectures and talks on asthma prevention and management. The experimental group (Group 2) received five one-hour sessions on how to control and manage asthma actively. Here activities involved developing mastery skills, and changes to the home environment.

RESULTS Both groups were shown to have an increased knowledge of asthma. Those children in Group 2 (the experimental group) showed higher levels of adherence and lower levels of hospital treatments for asthma attacks than children in the control group.

CONCLUSION The research demonstrates that information alone about an illness has only a limited effect on the control a person has over it. Children need specific guidance on mastery skills to effectively control their illness.

REFLECTIVE Activity

Different illnesses attract different attitudes from other people. Think about the ways in which we view people with asthma, cancer, diabetes, and so on. Are there differences? For instance, how seriously do we take people with each illness or disease? Do we consider any of these as relatively unimportant? For example, in William Golding's novel *The Lord of the Flies*, one character has asthma, and is represented as somewhat soppy and weak. Do we still have these kinds of views now that asthma is more common than it was when Golding wrote the book?

EVALUATIVE COMMENT

Asthma attacks have been shown to result from a range of different causes. The three main factors or causes are: allergies, infections of the respiratory system, and psychosocial factors. Research by Lewis *et al.* (1984) demonstrates that the asthma sufferer can control the degree and number of attacks, and manage their condition better after an attack. Health psychologists have a key role to play here in giving individuals skills so that they feel able and can exert self-control over their condition.

2.5 Chronic and terminal illnesses

Chronic illness

What is chronic illness? By definition, chronic illness is not something that is easily cured. It is long-lasting, and is usually permanent. It is a condition that becomes part of a person's life. To some people, chronic illness is a part of life that they accept; to others it is a devastating thing, which makes their lives feel less valuable. Which reaction occurs depends upon the personality of the individual, the support they require and whether this is matched by the support they receive, and the severity of the illness. Common chronic illnesses include diabetes, arthritis, heart disease, asthma and Crohn's disease (which affects the digestive tract).

A terminal illness, by contrast, is one that will ultimately lead to death. Doctors do not have the capacity to cure such illnesses, so all that can be done is to hope that the illness is defeated by the body's defence mechanisms (quite a rare thing), and to reduce any pain or suffering. Some chronic illnesses are essentially terminal, although if they are likely to cause death over many years rather than a shorter period of time, we are more likely to view them as chronic illness. Therefore, we call heart disease a chronic illness, even though it is commonly the cause of death in those people who have it.

There are some similarities between terminal and chronic illnesses, one being a person's reaction to being told what is wrong with them. On diagnosis, Shontz (1975) describes a set of stages through which people may seem to pass. Initially there is *shock* upon hearing the diagnosis. This is considerably more profound when the diagnosis was entirely unexpected – for example, when a person with a persistent thirst but no other symptoms is told they have diabetes. Following this, the patient may undergo an *encounter reaction*, involving many negative feelings, distress and possibly anger. The third phase, known as *retreat*, is essentially denial, where the patient acts as if the disease or illness is simply not present, is not happening to them. Eventually the patient leaves these stages and comes to terms with the illness (this is summarised in Figure 2.7). These stages are not set in stone: some people will not show any reaction that is clearly classifiable as one of these in isolation, others show a blend of them at any one time.

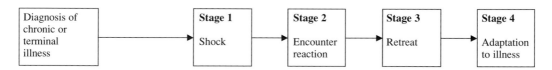

Figure 2.7: Four-stage model, proposed by Schontz (1975), to show the stages an individual goes through upon learning about a chronic or terminal illness

A common reaction to a diagnosis is to ascribe blame, often self-blame. In many illnesses, people look for a reason why they have succumbed to it. People will look to environmental exposures or to their own lack of self-care. They may lay the blame at the door of those around them.

EVALUATIVE COMMENT

There is a very mixed literature on this issue: some researchers claim that self-blame is harmful to the individual, some that it is a coping strategy with positive aspects to it, and others that it has little effect on anything. As research progresses, we may be able to identify individuals for whom self-blame may be positive and for whom it may be negative, with a view to modifying

such a perception of causation. **An example of self-blame working for the good of the individual comes from Hampson (1997). She showed that self-blame is a common causative explanation of diabetes, and that diabetics who self-blame are often those who demonstrate greatest control over their illness. This makes some sense – if a person thinks that their behaviours have caused their illness, they ought also to believe that they are capable of controlling it themselves and managing it too.**

Condition	Biomedical intervention	Psychological intervention
Asthma	Drugs to open the airways. Drugs to control the immune system where allergy is suspected.	Cognitive-behavioural approaches to teach the person to avoid asthma-causing behaviours and to reduce negative thoughts and panic.
Cancer	Surgery to remove affected tissue, and radiotherapy/chemotherapy to kill affected tissue.	Reducing negative thoughts, increasing positive thoughts, increasing coping. Also imagery, such as thinking of the body as an army fighting the disease.
Diabetes	Dietary control and giving insulin to make up for the body's deficits.	Help with lifestyle changes such as dietary control.
Coronary heart disease (CHD)	Drugs to thin the blood, surgery to remove blockages from veins and arteries, bypasses and heart transplants.	Help with lifestyle changes such as eating better, taking exercise, and giving up alcohol and tobacco.
HIV/AIDS	Antiviral drugs to keep illnesses at bay and boost the immune system.	Help with coping, social support, and help with lifestyle changes.

Figure 2.8: Biomedical and psychological therapies for chronic and terminal illnesses

Coronary heart disease

Coronary heart disease (CHD) is a term used to refer to hardening of the arteries that work with the heart in pumping blood around the body. Clumps of fat build up in the arteries and these deposits harden over time, causing the arteries to be less elastic and also narrowing them, restricting blood flow. It can be caused by a number of things, particularly smoking and eating high-fat foods. CHD is the principal cause of death in the UK and many other countries, and so is an area of high interest for doctors and psychologists alike. Doctors can give drugs and perform surgery to assist in the disease, and psychologists can help people to change their lifestyles to protect themselves.

Psychologists can work with patients in reducing smoking and in changing their diets, but there are other ways in which they can help. One risk factor is stress plus another Type A behaviour; this is explained in more detail in Chapter 4. By changing people's reactions to stress, and by modifying the characteristics of the **Type A personality**, they can, in theory, reduce the risks of CHD. However, we should remember that there are some who believe that Type A behaviour is 'built in' to the personality, and of course it is harder to change a personality than a behaviour. More recent research has cast doubt on the relationship between CHD and Type A behaviour.

Study 2.8

AIM Johnston *et al.* (1987) conducted a study to investigate whether or not there is a relationship between Type A behaviour and coronary heart disease.

METHOD Nearly 6000 men aged between 40 and 59 years of age were examined for signs of heart disease and had Type A behaviour measured by a questionnaire developed by Bortner (1969). Each person was followed up for an average of six years.

RESULTS While manual workers were found to have higher scores for Type A behaviour compared to non-manual workers, no relationship between Type A behaviour and CHD was found.

CONCLUSION Research has been mixed in the evidence that has and has not been found relating Type A behaviour to heart disease. No clear, compelling link seems to exist.

Some psychologists now think that **hostility** might be a better measure. Hostile people are similar to Type A people, but not the same. Hostility is simply one characteristic of Type A behaviour, and is essentially a kind of anger at other people and other things, and a willingness to dislike others. Because it is just one personality dimension, it might be easier to change than the full range of factors that make up Type A behaviour.

EVALUATIVE COMMENT

Miller *et al.* (1996) conducted a meta-analysis of 15 studies into the link between hostility and coronary heart disease. Meta-analyses are special statistical analyses of collections of studies. Instead of doing a piece of new research, it is possible to take all of the existing research into a particular topic and then add it all together to make one big study that can be analysed in one go. The advantage of this is that one can achieve very large sample sizes. If ten studies are added together, each with 1000 participants, the meta-analysis deals with 10,000 participants, which leads to a stronger result in statistical terms. Miller *et al.* found that, overall, there was a strong link between hostility and CHD. They argued that social support may play a part in this. We know that social support can help to fend off the effects of other factors. Having friends is good for our health. Of course, hostile individuals might not have many friends, because they are unfriendly people!

THE ROLE OF PSYCHOLOGY IN CORONARY HEART DISEASE

Health psychology plays an important role in both the prediction of coronary heart disease and helping to change the behaviour of a person to reduce risk of future CHD. In addition, health psychologists have an increasingly important role in creating and implementing rehabilitation programmes for people who have suffered CHD. This is summarised in Figure 2.9.

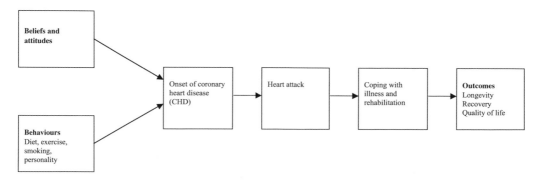

Figure 2.9: The role of health psychology in the onset, treatment and coping stages of coronary heart disease (adapted from Ogden, 2000: 314)

Cancer

Cancer (neoplasm) is the development of abnormal cells in the body. It can occur in any tissue, including bone or blood cells. It can be benign, which means that it is relatively harmless and will not spread, or it can be malignant. Malignant neoplasms are prone to spreading by cells leaving the tumour and moving elsewhere in the body (known as metastasis).

Cancer is another major area of study by health psychologists of chronic illness. It affects about one-third of us, eventually. It is an interesting disease since it bridges the gap between chronic illness and **palliative care**. Not all people with cancer die from it by any means. When cancer is not terminal, it is often a chronic illness, since it may take years to be treated successfully. Freud himself, for instance, spent many years struggling against cancer of the mouth in the last 20 years of his life. However, when cancer defeats both doctors and patients, it is then a case for palliative care (care that supports people who have a terminal illness).

Cancer results in strong emotional reactions, especially since it affects so many people. Most of us know someone who has died of cancer, and many of us will know people who have had cancer but have survived it. It is an emotive subject not just for patients, but for their families and their doctors and nurses too.

Study 2.9

AIM Wilkinson (1991) investigated how nurses communicate with cancer patients.

METHOD Nurse communication style was analysed and assigned to one of four categories: facilitators, ignorers, informers, and mixers. Mixers were nurses who showed facilitatory skills and who also ignored at times.

RESULTS 'Facilitators' were found to help patients express their fears and concerns about their cancer and its consequences. 'Ignorers' avoided cues from patients and did not want to be drawn into conversation about the patient's cancer. 'Informers' mainly gave facts about the cancer to the patient. 'Mixers' used an ignoring strategy at times to avoid difficult issues raised by patients (such as, 'How long will I live?').

CONCLUSION No one strategy is the best since nurses have also to cope with their own emotional responses and feelings. Generally the 'mixer' communication style may be most effective for both patient and nurse.

EVALUATIVE COMMENT

Why this occurs is understandable, but it is far from ideal. The emotional drain on nurses caused by dealing with patients' feelings is damaging to their own health, at least in principle, and with limited resources nurses are simply prioritising. This is a good example of where a health psychologist or counsellor can be of use in health services. Since nurses may lack communication skills in these cases, and lack time, there is an argument for using the skills of other professionals to plug the gap.

What, then, do cancer patients feel? They experience a range of emotions, as one would expect, and their histories and personalities will affect these. There is some evidence, also, to show that the course of their illness interacts with their emotions and cognitions. Some research has suggested that there is a **Type C personality**. Just as there has been work directed at identifying types of people who are most likely to develop heart disease (the Type A/Type B distinction), there is also some evidence that some people are more prone to developing cancer than others, the so-called Type C personality (Temoshok, 1987). The Type C person tends to repress their emotions rather than give vent to them. In this respect, they are the opposite of the Type A person. They do not tend to express anger, they do not forgive others easily, but they work hard to fit in with others and give in to their requirements. They are co-operative, even when their own needs conflict with those of others. Some have suggested that they indulge in self-pity more than average, that they lack social support networks because they tend to be loners, and that they often have a poor self-image. Many psychologists are sceptical about the cancer-predisposing personality, but a study by Shaffer *et al.* (1987) suggests that there is such a thing. Almost 1000 doctors were tracked over three decades, and those who gave vent to their feelings were 16 times less likely to develop cancer than those who 'bottled up' their feelings.

EVALUATIVE COMMENT

This study did not suffer from the flaw that has dogged research into personality and health in general: many studies look at people after they have developed an illness, assess their personalities, and then compare them to a control group. Of course, illness can change personality. The only effective way to approach this particular topic is to assess a large number of people, and then wait until they become ill during the natural course of their lives, looking for trends in disposition as disease develops. This is what Shaffer *et al.* (1987) did.

Some theorists suggest that the personality–cancer link works through psychoneuroimmunology. Basically, 'holding in' one's feelings causes stress, and stress suppresses the immune system. A suppressed immune system is less able to deal with the rogue cells that develop in our bodies quite regularly. When the rogue cells are not dealt with, they proliferate and become the disease cancer.

Treatments for cancer are themselves the source of a great deal of stress for patients. They rarely have a rapid effect and usually run over months or years. They involve intense nausea, weakness and loss of hair (essentially signs of radiation sickness, since radiation is used to treat cancer, even though it is one of its causes). Patients can, therefore, fall prey to feelings of cognitive dissonance (Festinger, 1957). They are being cared for and treated by doctors, but actually feel much worse than when they were not. At times, it can be difficult for them to believe that the additional pain caused by the treatment is worth it. Since the treatment causes nausea, they can often start to develop a conditioned response. As a result, various factors in their environment start to make them feel ill just because they associate them with the treatment (Jacobsen *et al.*, 1993). However, people do expect treatments to have side-effects, especially those for cancer, about which they may have heard a great deal. Leventhal *et al.* (1986) found that women with breast cancer were anxious about their chemotherapy because it did not have significant side-effects. They equated this with the treatment's perceived lack of power, and were concerned that they were not having their cancer treated with the most potent therapy available.

Cancer presents an unusual post-treatment threat, since unlike other illnesses or diseases there is always a concern that it might return, only for the patient to have to undergo anxiety-provoking tests and treatments all over again. There is evidence to show that the psychological distress caused by a diagnosis of recurrent cancer is greater than that generated by the original diagnosis.

EVALUATIVE COMMENT

Research into coping with cancer has found that 'fighting spirit' is important. For some people, denial is an effective strategy. Pettingale *et al.* (1985) found a survival advantage of five to ten years in breast cancer patients who denied or fought their illness after diagnosis. As Salmon (2000) asserts, however, the relationship between a coping strategy and survival is a correlational one, which does not necessarily imply direct causation. Other factors might pin together these two. For instance, fighting spirit can lead to better nursing care, which leads to better survival. If you are a 'fighter', the staff may like you more. You might eat more, to help you fight the disease. Or, a predisposition to surviving cancer might be provided by a gene that is also linked to having a fighting-spirit personality. However, as Dunkel-Schetter *et al.* (1992) found, over a half of patients with cancer did not have a main coping strategy. We might think,

at first, that this is a bad thing, but we must remember that a person who does not have a main coping strategy may use a mixture of strategies to cope, and is perhaps better off than someone who relies on one strategy for all eventualities.

CHRONIC ILLNESS AND CONTROL

Much of what has been said about chronic illness centres around the issue of control. Generally, patients who feel in control of their illness cope better than those who feel, in contrast, that they are somehow at the mercy of it or not in control. Fighting spirit cannot exist without some sense of personal control, and many other coping strategies rely upon the individual controlling both their own thoughts and behaviours. Self-management of treatment regimes is achieved more easily when a person believes that doing so is within their grasp. However, control is not always a good thing. Pain relief, used for many chronic illnesses, such as cancer or arthritis, can be handed over to the patient. This is known as patient-controlled analgesia (PCA), and can involve administering direct injections of painkillers into a vein via a machine the patient controls. This not only gives the patient a hand in managing their own symptoms, but also frees up the time of the health professionals, who would otherwise have to administer the analgesia. Research indicates that control is not always the important issue, but simply gaining access to pain relief when it is required. Since doctors and nurses are not always available, patients suffer until they are. PCA prevents this occurring, since when pain relief is needed, pain relief is available. Patients do not seem to care who does the job, as long as it is done (Taylor *et al.*, 1996).

Control can take a number of forms. Taylor *et al.* (1984) looked at the relationship between control and adjustment to breast cancer, comparing a number of types of control. Cognitive control seemed to be associated with the most adjustment, which is thinking about the cancer and life differently and 'filing away' negative ideas in a neat fashion. Interestingly, there was no relationship between adjustment to breast cancer and informational control. This means that having knowledge about breast cancer from information leaflets and the like did not assist the women in coming to terms with their disease. This suggests that information can, at times, simply increase fear, especially reading about the probabilities of your own death, or treatments that involve a lot of discomfort.

There are documented cases of people surviving a diagnosis of terminal illness. These may represent a good opportunity for health psychologists to examine the power that the mind has over the bodily mechanisms.

Study 2.10

AIM Greer (1991) identified a survival characteristic associated with the coping style first referred to by Derogatis *et al.* (1979): 'fighting spirit'.

METHOD In a 15-year study, 62 women were followed up after a diagnosis of breast cancer. Five reactions were identified; these were fighting spirit, stoic acceptance, helplessness/hopelessness, anxious preoccupation, and denial. Denial needs no explanation. Anxious preoccupation is a greater-than-normal level of worry and focus on the cancer. Helplessness/hopelessness is exactly what it sounds like. Stoic acceptance is taking a philosophical stance, almost like that of the existentialist philosophers – taking on board the diagnosis as part of life and accepting it, since it is what it is. Those with fighting spirit are the people who accept the diagnosis, but refuse to let cancer 'beat them'. They fight the illness, using all their resources.

RESULTS After 15 years, almost half of the women who were characterised by the 'fighting spirit' reaction were alive, compared with less than a fifth in the other coping-style groups.

CONCLUSION This seems to suggest that fighting an illness, which is largely a psychological response, pays dividends. Research into 'fighting spirit', however, remains balanced; there are studies both for and against its protective effect.

Acquired immune deficiency syndrome (AIDS)

The human immunodeficiency virus (HIV) transmits itself largely through contact between people via blood, vaginal mucus and/or semen in any combination. The presence of wounds in the mouth, on the genitals, and so on, can increase its likelihood of transmission, especially sexually. In many countries, such as the UK, AIDS has not become the epidemic that some people were predicting decades ago, partly due to the success of campaigns to warn people of the dangers of unprotected sexual intercourse, and perhaps partly due to medical advances, which have meant that HIV infection is much less likely to lead to AIDS than it was when the disease was new to doctors. However, in many countries, Africa in particular, HIV infection is widespread (with around 80 per cent of the world's HIV-infected people living in Africa). A combination of poverty, poor nutrition, lack of education about sexual health, high rates of prostitution (linked, of course, to poverty) and lack of medical resources can be blamed for this. If people cannot afford condoms and have not been told how HIV infection occurs, it is not surprising that the rates of transmission are high. In places where prostitution is one of a very small number of ways in which women (and men, of course) can make money to clothe, feed and protect their families, the HIV virus is more likely to be able to spread.

Mays and Cochran (1988) point out that the perceived risk from HIV infection and AIDS is, to many people, just one more risk in a world full of them. Their study of black and Hispanic American women showed that AIDS was not a particular fear for them over and above the other social, political and financial threats such women often face as part of their daily lives. Therefore, in a rank ordering of challenges and threats, AIDS is often seen as a relatively distant one. This kind of logic clearly explains the fact that people who are prostitutes out of financial necessity may be willing to engage in unprotected sex with their clients. Sex without condoms usually attracts a higher fee than sex with them. The reasoning behind this may be as follows: 'If I do this, I *might* get infected with HIV. Chances are that this one encounter will not infect me, but it's a possibility. But I *will* get money for this, and I need money. I can be certain of feeding my family for the next week. If I don't feed my children, they *will* get ill and they *will* be taken away from me.' Such priority-setting behaviour is, therefore, understandable in the circumstances. Another situation where risk-taking may occur is when drugs are involved. When sex is offered in exchange for drugs, HIV infection is often a minor consideration (Booth *et al.*, 1991).

Psychology has been shown to play a role in the susceptibility of people to the HIV virus. Psychological factors such as lifestyle, use of drugs and contraction of other sexual illnesses seem to increase a person's risk (Lifson *et al.*, 1989). Psychology has also been shown to feature in the progression from HIV to AIDS. Both lifestyle and the psychological state of a person are seen as key psychological factors (Ogden, 2000). Stress factors such as bereavement may also hasten progression from HIV to AIDS.

Study 2.11

AIM Reed *et al.* (1999) studied 72 men who were HIV-positive to investigate the role of bereavement in the progression to AIDS.

METHOD Half of the 72 men had recently experienced the death of someone close to them (friend, partner, etc.), the other half had not. The 72 men were followed up for a six-year period.

RESULTS The men who had experienced the death of someone close to them showed higher rates of progression to AIDS than those who had not experienced a bereavement.

CONCLUSION Negative emotional experiences, such as those caused by bereavement, seem to lead to AIDS progression faster than if someone who is HIV-positive does not have a major negative emotional experience.

EVALUATIVE COMMENT

Psychologists employ a range of interventions to help people reduce their risk of becoming HIV-positive, to manage their symptoms, and help cope with major life stresses in order to delay as long as possible the progression from HIV to AIDS. Psychologists also offer counselling and other psychological therapies to promote healthy living and behaviour to combat AIDS.

REFLECTIVE Activity

Doctors have to consider all aspects of a patient's case, not just their illness. A good doctor thinks about a patient's life too. If you were a doctor, you might have to tell a patient that they are HIV-positive. Not only would you have to deal with their reactions, you would also have to think about their partner, and whether it was likely they too had been infected. What if the patient told you that they had been unfaithful to their partner, and this was how they had become infected? Make a list of all the ethical issues you think this would give rise to, and think of how you might give advice.

2.6 Sample questions

SAMPLE QUESTION

(a)   Identify and outline two practitioner styles.

(AO1 = 4)   *(4 marks)*

(b)   Identify and explain one reason why patients may not comply with medical advice.

(AO1 = 2, AO2 = 2)   *(4 marks)*

(c)   Discuss two psychological interventions that can be used with either CHD or AIDS sufferers.

(AO1 = 4, AO2 = 8)   *(12 marks)*

Total AO1 marks = 10   Total AO2 marks = 10   Total = 20 marks

QUESTIONS, ANSWERS AND COMMENTS

(a)   Identify one self-report measure of pain and explain one limitation of this method.

(AO1 = 1, AO2 = 2)   *(3 marks)*

(b)   Describe one study in which patient – practitioner communication was investigated. Include in your answer why the study was conducted, the method used, results obtained and conclusions drawn.

(AO1 = 5)   *(5 marks)*

(c)   Discuss two factors that are thought to affect patients' compliance with medical advice. Refer to empirical evidence in your answer.

(AO1 = 4, AO2 = 8)   *(12 marks)*

Total AO1 marks = 10   Total AO2 marks = 10   Total = 20 marks

Answer to (a)

One method of measuring pain is to use the McGill Pain Questionnaire (MPQ). This measures four different dimensions of pain; these are the location of the pain, how the pain feels, direction of the pain over time and the intensity of the pain. The intensity of the pain is measured by asking people to choose 'pain words' from a list provided. One limitation of the MPQ is that people may not be truthful about the pain they are experiencing. A person, for other reasons, may seek to make their pain seem worse or better than it is.

Comment: The answer provides a full description of the MPQ and so would gain the one AO1 mark available for the question (however the description is probably too full for just one mark).

The limitation identified is acceptable, and the reason a person may not tell the truth when self-reporting is expanded on. Hence, the two AO2 marks available would be awarded. This answer would score the full three marks.

Answer to (b)

AIM Hall *et al.* (1994) conducted a study to look at the role of the gender of the doctor in doctor – patient communication.

METHOD Female and male doctors were observed making communications to patients.

RESULTS Female doctors were found to make more positive statements, asked more questions and enquired more about a patient's relationship with other people than male doctors.

CONCLUSION Female doctors talk about different things with their patients than male doctors.

Comment: The answer is reasonably clear and precisely stated and would attract one mark. The method description is inadequate and would get no marks. Information about numbers of doctors, types and numbers, and gender of patients is needed. The results are clearly and specifically stated. The conclusion is vague and inadequate. This would score three out of the five marks available.

Answer to (c)

Two factors that psychologists have researched in patient compliance are, first, understanding of the information and, second, trust in the doctor. If a patient does not understand the nature of their illness and the reason why it is important to stick to the pill-taking requirement on the prescription, then adherence may not be high. Compliance is not used so much in the health psychology literature or by health psychologists these days. The term 'adherence' is more popular since the word implies that people have free will to choose to do what the doctor asks of them. In contrast, the word 'compliance' sounds more authoritative and puts the doctor more in the role of giving orders. Health psychologists have conducted research to show that this approach does not work that well. Bandura's concept of self-efficacy may explain this difference between adherence and compliance. McAuley (1993) showed that high self-efficacy (the belief that you can do something) in people was related to adhering to a healthy fitness programme. Tedesco *et al.* (1991) found that dental advice to look after your teeth was more likely to be followed in people with high self-efficacy.

Trust in the doctor is very important because if you do not trust your doctor then you may think he has prescribed the wrong pills for you. In consequence, you will not take the pills if you think they are wrong for the illness that you have.

Comment: The candidate correctly identifies two factors that may affect compliance with medical advice. The discussion on compliance and adherence is relevant, although this could be focused on more clearly in relation to the types of communication between the doctor and the patient. The concept of self-efficacy is also relevant to the concept of adherence, and relevant empirical evidence is provided. The discussion on the second factor of trust is subjective and contains no reference to concepts or research in health psychology. Overall this answer would get seven out of the 12 marks available; of these seven marks, four would be for AO1 and three for AO2. To improve more on the second factor of trust from a health psychology perspective is needed, together with a clearer structure for the whole essay answer.

2.7 FURTHER READING

Introductory texts

Ogden, J. 2000: **Health Psychology: A Textbook**. 2nd Ed. Chapters 4, 8, 11 and 13. Open University Press, Buckingham

Sarafino, E.P. 2002: **Health Psychology**. 4th Ed. Chapters 9, 11 and 13. John Wiley & Sons, New York

Specialist sources

Blackwell, B. 1997: From compliance to alliance: a quarter century of research, in B. Blackwell (ed.) **Treatment Compliance and Therapeutic Alliance**. Harwood Academic Publishers, Amsterdam

Bonica, J.J. (ed.) 1990: **The Management of Pain**. 2nd Ed. Lea & Febiger, Philadelphia

Rhodes, T. and Hartnell, R. 1986: **AIDS, Drugs and Prevention: Perspectives on Individual and Community Action**. Routledge, London

3

Lifestyles and health

3.1 Aspects of healthy living

It may seem obvious, but for health psychologists it is health that is a key concern, rather than illness. Therefore, anything that can lead to and maintain health is likely to be researched by health psychologists. Some people, we can suggest, have healthy lifestyles, and some people have lifestyles that actually discourage health and lead to illness (physical and psychological). A healthy lifestyle involves exercise, a balanced diet, having friends, and – unfortunate but true – having money. This chapter examines some of these factors and how they contribute to health.

Exercise is beneficial, provided that it is the right kind of exercise for the right kind of person

Exercise

Exercise is good for you, so it is said. However, like everything in life, things are not quite so simple. All forms of exercise are not recommended for all people, and just as a person should walk before they run, so they should build up an exercise regime starting with mild exercise. Furthermore, again like anything else, too much of a good thing can be a bad thing. A person who exercises too much may become addicted to the exercise, and will eventually wear their body down and, for example, put excess strain upon their heart. Those people who seem to live in the gym may be doing themselves more harm than good. However, a moderate amount exercise is good for people, just as a moderate amount of socialising is, and a moderate amount of fat, carbohydrate and other foodstuffs.

Exercise is linked to fitness. However, not all forms of exercise lead to increased fitness, because we tend to define fitness in a particular way. Fitness is our ability to burn up sugars in the body to release energy and use the oxygen in our blood to help this to occur. Fitness, therefore, involves breathing. A fit person breathes well, and their muscles work well in using the body's fuel to create energy. As you will see later, exercise that makes us breathe quickly and heavily leads to the best levels of fitness, unlike exercise such as weight-lifting, which tends to involve lots of energy but not sustained deep breathing.

REFLECTIVE Activity

Think about the different types of exercise you get and, if appropriate, any special exercise you engage in. How often do you exercise? How fit and healthy do you feel? How much more (or less) exercise do you think you should do compared to what you do at present?

What forms of exercise are there? Those people who study exercise and its effects on the body (including physiologists and sports psychologists) classify exercise as follows: aerobic, anaerobic, isotonic, isometric and isokinetic. These are summarised in Figure 3.1.

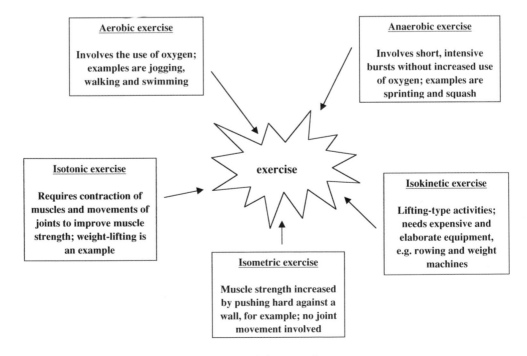

Figure 3.1: Five types of exercise, with examples

AEROBIC EXERCISE

Essentially, aerobic exercise involves oxygen. Muscles can work in two ways: with or without oxygen. When a person takes part in aerobic exercise, a lot of oxygen is used along with the sugars in the blood to make the muscles work. Essentially, the fitter someone is the more able their body is to use the oxygen efficiently in this process. Those who study body chemistry know a lot about these processes, but health psychologists need only understand the very basics, since they are not closely concerned with what is happening in the body, but focus mainly on what is happening in the mind. With aerobic exercise, intensity and duration are important. The exercise should increase heart rate, but not to very high levels, for a period of 10 to 20 minutes. Cooper (1985) recommends exercise of this sort for five days a week.

ANAEROBIC EXERCISE

Anaerobic exercise works without the use of oxygen. It is the body's way of allowing a person to take part in sudden, aggressive and temporary activities, in nature primarily to avoid danger. It takes the body a little while to pump oxygen around, and time might be limited if a tiger is chasing an animal, or you are running to cross the road with a car zooming towards you. In these cases, the muscles have to work, even if the oxygen is not yet available. The body cannot sustain anaerobic exercise for very long. It is a temporary measure. When athletes take part in a 100 m sprint, they rely partly on anaerobic exercise because the race is so short and the amount of energy expended so high. They do not have the luxury of the time to take lots of breaths. However, even the best athletes cannot run at that speed for much longer than the ten seconds it takes to finish the race. If they were to try, they would collapse. The body would 'switch off' to prevent death.

ISOTONIC EXERCISE

This is a type of exercise that helps to increase strength, but also to increase endurance, by means of the body using force in a single direction. It is achieved through moving an object, either the body itself or some kind of weight. Examples include things such as weight-lifting, or even pushing a broken-down car.

ISOMETRIC EXERCISE

In this form of exercise, strength is increased, but not usually endurance. It involves force applied to an object that will not move. Many muscle-building exercises intended to be performed without expensive equipment take this form. For example, if you place your palms together in front of your chest and then push, your muscles will be working hard, but they will balance each other out, so that your arms will remain in a stationary position. Arm wrestling with someone who has exactly the same strength as you will, in theory, result in nothing happening. In the example above of a broken-down car, trying to push it with the handbrake on will convert isotonic exercise into isometric exercise.

ISOKINETIC EXERCISE

This is a form of exercise that involves opposing sets of muscles. When you push open a door, the muscles you use are different from those used when you pull it open towards you. Try this and you will feel the muscles working. Rowing is an example of this in real sport. Sawing wood is another example. In the case of our broken-down car, imagine pushing it forwards a little and then pulling it back towards you, then pushing it forwards again, and so on. This type of exercise is better than isometric and isotonic in building muscle strength and muscle endurance.

REFLECTIVE Activity

Make a list of common sports and exercise activities, then try to identify which ones involve which types of exercise listed above. You may find that they overlap.

Exercise should be carried out in moderation, carefully, and ideally when other people are present. Too much exercise will damage the body, and if accidents do occur it is best if someone is there to help. In terms of what exercise can do for a person psychologically, there is biological evidence that it can help to kill pain and make them feel happy. Evidence from research has shown the benefits of regular exercise.

Study 3.1

AIM King *et al.* (1997) conducted a study with people reporting problems with sleeping, to investigate the benefits of exercise.

METHOD Sedentary men and women, aged between 50 and 76 years of age who reported moderate sleep complaints took part in the study. Members of a control group were placed in a 'waiting list' and not asked to take additional exercise. The experimental group engaged in 40 minutes of fast walking four times a week for 16 weeks.

RESULTS Those in the experimental group showed improvements in their sleep patterns; they fell asleep more quickly and their time spent asleep increased.

CONCLUSION Exercise on a regular but not over-exerting basis improves sleep patterns.

Other research has shown that exercise may help to alleviate feelings of depression (Stein and Motta, 1992) in, for example, elderly males and females in a residential nursing home, and in students and pregnant women. However, for people who suffer from clinical depression, the research evidence is more mixed, with some research showing improvement from regular running as a form of exercise.

Study 3.2

AIM Bosscher (1993) investigated the effects of exercise on people suffering from clinical depression.

METHOD Depressed patients were randomly assigned to a control group where no special treatment was given, or to an experimental group. Those in the experimental group took part in a short-term running schedule.

RESULTS Patients in the experimental group showed raised levels of self-esteem and lower levels of the symptoms of depression. Those in the control group showed no changes.

CONCLUSION Running may help to reduce the symptoms of depression in clinically depressed people.

EVALUATIVE COMMENT

Martinsen and Morgan (1997) reviewed research on the effectiveness of exercise as a treatment for clinical depression. They concluded that aerobic exercise was beneficial, but only for relatively mild forms of depression. In severely depressed people exercise seems to have little beneficial effect. Martinsen and Morgan (1997) also noted that exercise, largely aerobic in nature, may have beneficial effects for unipolar and mild-to-moderate depression, but not severe or bipolar depression. Exercise has also been shown to be of benefit in reducing levels of anxiety (Raglin, 1997) and can act as a buffer against stress (Sonstroem, 1997). Finally, exercise may also be of benefit in increasing self-esteem especially where someone suffers from low self-esteem (Sonstroem, 1997).

While exercise may have valuable effects on health by reducing anxiety, feelings of depression and stress, and increasing self-esteem, it may also have negative effects. Athletes who overtrain have been found to suffer from negative moods, mild depression and fatigue (O'Connor, 1997). Some people become addicted to exercise to such an extent that it disrupts their normal life and interferes with work and domestic activities (Glasser, 1976). Conboy (1994) showed that people addicted to running actually exhibit withdrawal symptoms if they stop running. These withdrawal symptoms included restlessness, tension, anxiety and guilt. Slay *et al.* (1998) have shown that people addicted to running have unhealthy concerns about their body image and are obsessed with weight control. Excessive physical exercise may also cause numerous physical injuries (Cooper, 1982).

Nutrition: diet and ill-health

Without food and drink, we die. It makes sense that over millions of years of evolution we have developed an overriding requirement to feed ourselves. Of course, food comes in many forms, and there are good and bad diets. Eating high-fat foods is generally bad for our health, and eating fruit and vegetables is generally good for it. Most of what health psychologists study in the realm of nutrition is to do with the reasons why people eat what they eat.

Many societies around the world face a growing problem of **obesity**. As many as 14 per cent of people in England (Seidell and Rissenen, 1998) are clinically overweight, to a degree that doctors believe can be damaging to health in the long term. A heavier society is one that relies more upon health services, which costs more money. Naturally, then, there is a significant incentive for governments and health authorities to try to create slimmer, healthier nations. Bear in mind, however, that to suggest that obese people should be slimmer *for any reason other than health* is not acceptable. Obesity is a health issue to psychologists, not an issue of physical beauty.

DIET AND CARDIOVASCULAR DISORDERS

People who suffer from cardiovascular disorders, such as having had a heart attack, are advised by health psychologists to modify risk of future coronary heart disease through changes to diet, alcohol intake and stress (Ogden, 2000). People who are overweight or obese, and those with high levels of cholesterol are more likely to die of heart disease. Ogden (2000) suggests that those with very high cholesterol levels are three times more likely to die of heart disease than those with low levels of cholesterol. Cholesterol levels are determined by the amount of saturated fats in a person's diet. High intakes of saturated fats from eating butter, cheese, eggs and fatty meat such as burgers or sausages will cause a person to have high cholesterol levels. Levels of this substance may be reduced by eating more fibre, fruit and vegetables, and fewer saturated-fatty foods.

It is a common belief that obesity is associated with coronary heart disease (CHD). This is true to the extent that an obese person eats high-fat foods. Hence research by health psychologists has suggested that being overweight is much less of a risk factor per se than high-fat diets and high cholesterol levels (Trevisan *et al.*, 1990). Consuming high levels of vitamins, especially vitamin E has been shown to reduce the risk of cardiovascular disorders.

Study 3.3

AIM Stampfer *et al.* (1993) conducted a study to investigate whether or not taking vitamin E supplements reduced the risk of CHD.

METHOD Nurses and other health professionals were recruited for a longitudinal study, which took place over a two-year period. Participants were asked to take vitamin E on a regular basis over this time.

RESULTS Protective effects were not immediately apparent, however after two years of taking vitamin E nurses showed a decreased risk of cardiovascular disease.

CONCLUSION Regular consumption of vitamin E may have beneficial health effects and reduce the risk of heart disease.

EVALUATIVE COMMENT

Modifications to a person's diet through reducing levels of saturated fat intake, increasing dietary fibre and the intake of fruits and vegetables, together with vitamin supplements, helps protect a person against heart disease. However, other factors also increase the risks of cardiovascular disorders. These include smoking, high stress and anxiety levels, educational level and income, and low levels of social support (Brannon and Feist, 2000). Interestingly, emotions such as feelings of hostility and anger have been linked with heart disease. Overall, then, susceptibility to cardiovascular disorders, such as heart attack, may be increased by a poor diet (high fat intake) but other factors also need to be taken into account. Psychosocial risks include anxiety, lack of social support, living alone, hostility/anger and low income.

DIET AND CANCER

Research has provided some evidence that diet may affect susceptibility to cancer and that certain diets may offer some protection against cancer (Brannon and Feist, 2000). The American Cancer Society has estimated that diet plays a role in about one-third of all cancer deaths in the United States. The cancers that appear most related to diet include those of the breast, stomach, colon, kidneys, liver, prostate, mouth and oesophagus. Foods associated with cancer are those high in carcinogens; these include food additives, salt, smoked foods and 'old' food (due to their content of bacteria and fungi).

   Cancer of the colon has been especially associated with diet. Eating foods such as red meat, fast foods and low-fibre foods (refined foods), as well as high sugar intake, has been linked with cancer of the colon (Slattery *et al.*, 1998). Colonic cancer has been found to be lower where people eat high-fibre diets, have high vegetable and fruit intakes, and eat fish (oily) and poultry, with low intakes of red meat. Diet has also been shown to be related to lung cancer, especially high-cholesterol diets.

Study 3.4

AIM Shekelle *et al.* (1991) carried out a study over 24 years to investigate the relationship between diet and lung cancer.

METHOD Male workers at the Western Electric company were followed over 24 years. Food intakes and development of lung cancer were monitored in this large workforce.

RESULTS Men who had high cholesterol levels, and high intakes of fatty foods were found to have an increased incidence of lung cancer. Men with high fat levels were found to be twice as likely to contract lung cancer than those with lower fat levels.

CONCLUSION High cholesterol levels, especially derived from eggs, seem to be related to the risk of contracting cancer of the lung.

EVALUATIVE COMMENT

While diet, particularly cholesterol levels, may be associated with the risk of developing lung cancer, other factors, especially smoking, increase the risk much more. Smoking contributes to deaths from cardiovascular disorders and cancer. For lung cancer, around 80 to 90 per cent of deaths are associated with smoking (Heasinkveld, 1997). Diet may play a role in this type of cancer, but smoking has, it seems, an overriding effect.

   Certain types of diet may protect a person from getting cancer in the first place. Some connection, albeit weak, has been found between moderate intakes of vitamin A and decreased risk of lung and stomach cancer (Yong *et al.*, 1997). In addition, high levels of vitamin C intake have been found to protect against lung cancer (Yong *et al.*, 1997).

EVALUATIVE COMMENT

Evidence has been produced to show that low-intake levels of vitamins, such as A and E, and of trace elements such as selenium may increase cancer risk (Yong *et al.*, 1997). However, little evidence exists to support the taking of vitamin pills as a supplement to a healthy diet. A healthy diet, which includes high fibre intake, fruit, vegetables and whole grains, provides all the vitamins the body needs. Diets rich in animal fats, resulting in high cholesterol concentrations, do seem to be related to risk of cancer. Much more research is needed to ascertain more clearly the relationship between specific aspects of diet and specific types of cancer.

DIET AND DIABETES

Overweight people have a greater likelihood of developing *diabetes mellitus*. They tend not to live as long as people of statistically normal weight. They may have reduced self-image, which can lead to a loss of self-esteem (Miller and Downey, 1999). In this research, 71 studies of self-esteem measures and body weight were examined to show that the relationship between these factors was significant, and larger for women than for men. However, although statistically significant, the correlation is still relatively modest. There is certainly no obvious and direct 'gain weight–lose self-esteem' link.

DIET AND DEPRESSION

Foster *et al.* (1996) looked at depression in people over time and established that weight gains and losses were not associated with depressive episodes and remissions from depression. This contradicts the view that people who gain weight feel sad as a result. The problem with this type of research is that it overlooks individual differences in eating and emotional behaviour. Some people will not feel happy or sad in relation to their body shape or size. However, of those that

Research seems to indicate that taking vitamin pills as a supplement to a healthy diet does little to protect against cancer

do, some may become more depressed as a result of gaining weight, whereas others might gain weight as a result of depression due to some other cause (so-called 'comfort eating'). The various time-lags between eating behaviour and emotional reactions to weight gain and other life events may mean that there is no obvious relationship between body mass and depression when groups of people are looked at rather than individuals.

In addition, such studies tend to use tools to measure depression at clinical levels. Sub-clinical depression is more difficult to measure, but this is where body image might affect the obese person more. Becoming overweight might not make people clinically depressed – with all its common symptoms of changes in sleeping patterns, sociability, dietary habits, interest in life in general, and so on – but it might simply make them feel a little more sad or unhappy. We are currently less able to measure these small effects than we are full-scale depression.

Feeling good now can lead to feeling bad later

OVEREATING AND ILL-HEALTH

Why do people overeat? Why is it so difficult to lose weight and then to maintain a healthy proportion of body fat? The first question is likely to have numerous answers, and psychologists are only beginning to provide some of them, after many years of research. People may overeat, or at least may be overweight, because their culture and values tend to expect it. In Tonga, a very large proportion of people are overweight by western standards, and having excess body fat is the norm for both men and women. In some cultures, specifically those around and including India, being moderately overweight is perceived as a sign of riches, and in a man it is indicative of the fact that his wife is looking after him well. The meaning of 'being overweight' is, therefore, different around the world, and throughout time as values change. People may overeat because their bodies are constructed that way, either because their brains are 'set' that way or because they have more fat cells or a different metabolism to other people. Someone may overeat to provide comfort and reduce stress or boredom. People with a full social life, or a career where entertaining business clients is part of their job, may find themselves eating more because they have to go out to dinner and eat rich food more often.

REFLECTIVE Activity

Make a list of the situations where you eat more than usual, and those where you eat less. Think of the types of food you eat in each situation. Is there a pattern? Think also of how much choice you have in each situation over what you eat. Is it down to your own free will, or is what you are eating partly determined by your culture?

The view that some people seem to gain weight no matter how much they control their eating or that some people cannot gain weight no matter how much they eat, is partly borne out by research. A review of 29 studies on food intake by obese people did not show that overweight people ate more than people of normal weight (Spitzer and Rodin, 1981). However, the question we must ask is how much the overweight people are supposed to eat to maintain a normal body weight. It is quite possible that they are eating too much *for them*. The metabolic rates of individuals can have dramatic effects on body size. A person with a relatively fast and powerful heartbeat, for instance, may require more energy to maintain their heart's activity than a person with a relatively slow, weak one.

Over days and weeks of activity, this might add up to a considerable difference in energy requirements. Some people are generally more physically active than others, not just in obvious ways, such as in how much sport they engage in or what their work involves, but also in more subtle ways, such as how much they might thrash around in their sleep, or how much they talk in an average day, or how tense their muscles are in their basic resting state. If a person has slightly more tense muscles than another, this might mean that their body requires a little more

energy, even in its most relaxed state. Multiply this effect over years, and the difference in food consumed as a result might again be significant.

EVALUATIVE COMMENT

Herman and Mack (1975) categorised people into restrained eating and unrestrained eating. Restrained eaters are constantly conscious about what they eat and are careful to avoid certain foods. They may frequently be on calorie-controlled diets, and for them the business of eating can be a problematic one. They are the people who may report feeling 'guilty' after having the occasional chocolate bar, or who will, perhaps, miss a meal in order to make up for an additional slice of toast at breakfast. In contrast to this, the unrestrained eaters are people who simply eat what they like, when they like. They do not tend to count calories. You would be forgiven for thinking that unrestrained eaters are the people who become obese, but the relationship is far from being that simple. In fact, many theorists believe that unrestrained eating can be quite healthy and is nothing more than a form of 'listening' to the body's needs and supplying them by giving in to cravings and hunger. Restrained eaters, on the other hand, interfere with the body's natural processes by trying to alter and change their dietary habits.

Evidence that restraint leads to overeating comes from Wardle and Beales (1988). They took obese women and split them between three conditions; in one they were expected to engage in a low-calorie diet, another group was engaged in exercise, and a further group was simply enrolled into the study but given no instructions either to exercise or to diet. After a number of weeks, measures of food intake indicated that the women in the dieting condition actually ate more than the others.

Dieting and weight-loss techniques

Dieting is very big business. If you take a trip to a large bookshop you will find hundreds of books on dieting for health; these are usually aimed at those people who are overweight. They range from those books written on eating generally accepted healthy foods, to the more unusual, which suggest that some foods should only be eaten on certain days of the week or that certain foods should not be eaten together. Some of the more extreme diets, which are not usually recommended by nutritionists, may involve eating, for example, only carbohydrates or drinking only fruit juices over a period of a week.

The two main issues surrounding healthy diets tend to be addressed together in recommendations to their clients by nutritionists. Most healthy eating involves a reduction of fat and an increase in fibre. Fats are to be found in high quantities in 'junk food', cream, cheese, chocolate and animal fats, and although there are 'good fats' (unsaturated) which the body needs, most people in Britain consume too much of the 'bad' types of fat (saturated). Hand in hand with this is the fact that they often consume too little fibre, which is found in fruit and vegetables.

Most attempts by psychologists working with overweight individuals to modify eating behaviour, and thus achieve and maintain a normal body weight, ultimately fail (Garner and Wooley, 1991). Those people who manage to lose weight commonly start to gain weight again once the restrictive diet is over. However, being overweight can be such a health problem that it is simply not acceptable to give up trying to find ways to reduce the body fat of certain people. The lack of significant success over many years is not a reason to give up. Since it is so difficult to change the eating habits, and thus body weights, of obese people, many health researchers have concentrated their efforts on preventing people becoming obese in the first place. What is clear is that preventing children from becoming obese needs to involve the family, since poor eating habits could be learned at home. However, since there seems to be a strong genetic basis for obesity, with identical twins showing more similarities in weight than non-identical twins (Allison *et al.*, 1994), even the attempt to prevent children gaining weight might be associated with great difficulties.

We saw earlier that 'restrained' eaters are constantly aware of what they eat. This can be damaging both physically and psychologically. First, a restrained eater can disturb their body's metabolic processes by constantly trying out different diets and therefore rarely eating balanced and regular meals. Second, they can become obsessed by food, and this can lead to them having problems in life because they are unhappy with themselves and their eating habits. They might begin to lack self-esteem as a result.

Health psychologists are very interested in the distinction between restrained and unrestrained eaters because it is clearly a psychological way of dividing people in relation to their health-related behaviours. It is not something that doctors using medical approaches to weight loss can easily cure, because there seems to be something important about the personalities of people who differ in their eating habits. An important factor to consider about personality is that it is not easily changed. This is an essential problem for health psychologists generally, not just in relation to diet. If the distinction between restrained and unrestrained eaters is fundamentally all about their personalities, it is unlikely that psychologists can change this. Instead, they focus on altering behaviours. It is possible to change behaviour, and to change a person's thoughts and feelings about food. By doing so, any potentially harmful effects of personality can, in theory, be reduced.

BIOMEDICAL APPROACHES

Biomedical approaches to weight loss can range from the very mild to the very drastic. Doctors are able to change the metabolism of individuals using drugs, and can also suppress the appetite in the same way. Another way to change the body's reactions is to fill it up with bulky foods that contain very few calories, such as vegetables. The person feels full, so they stop eating, but they are slowly losing weight because they are not taking in large numbers of calories. The more extreme biomedical approaches include wiring up the mouth to stop people eating, stapling the stomach so that people feel full sooner because the stomach is smaller, and techniques such as liposuction, where the fat under the skin is sucked away surgically. Liposuction is not a long-term solution, however, because it does not change anything about the person. An individual who loves eating lots of food will do so as soon as they are able to, and will regain the weight removed by the surgical procedure.

Study 3.5

AIM Houston (1995) intended to discover if overweight women seeking stomach surgery to reduce their weight had different personalities from women who were of normal weight.

METHOD A personality questionnaire, the 16PF, was given to 230 obese women and to 55 normal-weight women. In addition, the women's ages and races were recorded to see if these factors might also influence interest in surgery to reduce obesity.

RESULTS No differences were found between the two groups of women on any of 15 of the 16 factors in the personality questionnaire. Age and race were also observed as not being important.

CONCLUSION There is no reason to assume that women who are overweight and want to reduce their weight by surgery are any different in personality from women of normal weight.

EVALUATIVE COMMENT

Health psychologists often want to find out if certain treatments appeal to certain types of people, and if those treatments actually work for particular people. People differ in many ways, and doctors aim to provide the best therapeutic approach for each of their patients. When psychologists are able to discover that specific treatments are best aimed at people with clearly defined personalities, a lot of time and money can be saved within health services.

Houston (1995) failed to find any differences in 15 personality factors between a group of obese women who were interested in having stomach surgery to decrease their weight and females of normal weight.

This highlights an important problem in researching these issues. When health psychologists investigate such things, they often do not know what factors are likely to be important, so they make educated guesses and they sometimes get it wrong. Houston's (1995) study is an example of this kind of exploratory approach. The fact that no differences between the groups were found is useful to researchers, however, because it allows them to identify what not to investigate in the future. Knowing what not to do is just as important as knowing anything else.

BEHAVIOURAL APPROACHES

There are many types of psychological approach to weight loss, all of which aim to change behaviour. Some of the popular and most successful techniques are those that rely upon **conditioning**. There are many examples of conditioning that might occur in a person's life. Indeed, some people argue that almost everything we do is underpinned by stimulus–response associations. For example, as children, we learn not to run across a busy road, because if we try to do this our parents may shout at us. We learn to associate the behaviour (running across the road) with an unpleasant outcome (being scolded) and as a consequence we think twice before doing it again.

Psychologists can use this pairing-up of a behaviour with something unpleasant to change eating behaviour. Have you ever been put off food by the thought of something horrible? Imagine tucking into a chocolate bar but thinking about soil while you do it. If you did this often enough you might actually start to think that chocolate tasted like soil. Of course, the benefits of this are obvious if someone is eating far too much chocolate and making themselves unhealthy because of it. This is an example of the application of classical conditioning to eating behaviour. The normal response to chocolate has been replaced by a different one. It is also possible to apply operant conditioning to weight loss behaviour too. If a person allows themselves 'rewards' for losing weight, they are using this principle. Just as a rat will learn to press a lever if it gets food for doing so, a person may learn to eat less if they reward themselves with a good book to read if they succeed in losing four pounds in a week, for example.

Study 3.6

AIM Cole and Bond (1983) aimed to discover if a programme of conditioning could help weight loss in women.

METHOD A total of 42 overweight women were enrolled in one of three conditions of the study. The experimental group was taught to associate the odours of certain selected foods with unpleasant smells. Over the eight weeks of the study four different unpleasant smells were used so that the women would not get used to the same odour over time. Another group was enrolled in the study but did not receive the pairing of food smells with unpleasant smells, but they did get to spend some time with the researchers. A third group was simply tracked over time and its members' weights measured.

RESULTS The researchers found that the experimental group lost an average of 4.7 pounds per person in weight over the course of the study; the group that simply spent time with the researchers lost 3.6 pounds; the group members that were simply weighed lost 0.5 pounds.

CONCLUSION The authors point out that this kind of therapy is of limited use compared with the social support that is provided by being enrolled in a study without receiving any conditioning treatment at all. However, both methods are significantly better than trying to lose weight alone.

EVALUATIVE COMMENT

Cole and Bond (1983) showed the moderate success of a treatment programme that involved pairing up the good smells of food with bad smells – like that of rotten eggs, for example. However, they also found that after a further period of time all groups who had lost weight gained it again. This is a common pattern of all weight-loss programmes of all types, not just those that rely on conditioning. In Cole and Bond's study, the treatment was not kept up, but ended at a particular time. Conditioning generally needs to be maintained for it to work. Once the desired foods were no longer paired up with bad smells, the people in the study probably found that their conditioned effects started to wear off. Second, all weight-loss treatments suffer from the fact that overeating may be learned in childhood, whereas dieting is something that adults are trying to do. Developmental psychologists have shown that behaviours learned in childhood are often extremely difficult to change, because they become part of the personality of the child, and therefore of the adult. This suggests that if we want to have a slimmer and healthier nation, we must try to teach healthy eating to children, before the 'bad habits' begin.

PRACTICAL Activity

Discuss with a group of friends the issues surrounding techniques of weight loss. First, identify a point at which you consider a person to need help with their eating behaviour. How fat do they have to be? Then, consider all the methods of weight loss – including the most extreme, such as stomach stapling – and make suggestions for how overweight someone needs to be before they should be offered each. What about you? If you needed help with your weight, what methods would you consider?

3.2 Changing health-related behaviour

Risk factors

We are surrounded by risk. It is a normal part of life. However, people often unnecessarily increase their risks by engaging in behaviours that can damage their bodies and perhaps even kill them. Health psychologists attempt to understand why people might do this. Eating a poor diet is one type of harmful behaviour, but there are many others, including smoking, high-risk sexual practices and alcohol abuse.

Smoking

In Britain in 1996, just under 30 per cent of people smoked (Office of National Statistics, 1999). The effects of smoking, and of passive smoking (ingesting other people's cigarette smoke from the air) are probably well known to you. You probably know that there is a relationship between smoking and lung disease such as lung cancer, for instance. Ask yourself how you know that. The answer is, partly, because health education and health-promotion campaigns can really work. Since the research into smoking first began to show that it is associated with health problems (US Department of Health, Education, and Welfare and US Public Health Service, 1964), health professionals around the world have been trying to get this message across to people. Of course, given that the anti-smoking ethos is so strongly supported in many countries, we must ask why so many people still smoke, and why so many young people take up the habit of smoking. Fifty or more years ago, people did not really know that smoking could be harmful. Now that most people do, why do they still do it?

We cannot deal here with every explanation of smoking that has ever been put forward in the history of psychology, since, for example, psychoanalytic theorists first suggested that smoking was a form of oral fixation. There are entire books on psychological aspects of smoking. Instead, we focus on a selection of these psychological explanations.

The content of tobacco cannot be ignored, since there is a strongly addictive element present: nicotine. Like any addictive substance, once people become used to having nicotine in their blood they crave it when it is absent or when levels fall too low. This view is known as the *nicotine-regulation model*, and was developed by Schachter (1977). However, this model fails to account for why people start smoking in the first place, or why some people smoke (albeit small amounts) even though they do not seem to be addicted in any measurable, physical sense; we call such smokers 'chippers' (Shiffman *et al.*, 1995). It is, therefore, important to look at psychological factors, especially prior to addiction itself having begun.

PSYCHOLOGICAL EXPLANATIONS OF SMOKING

It is likely that a combination of social, cultural, environmental and biological factors are involved in both uptake and maintenance of the habit of smoking. Most smokers begin the habit in their teenage years, a time when people are impressionable and open to peer pressure. Killen *et al.* (1997) have shown that having friends who smoke is significantly related to the likelihood of a person experimenting with smoking; indeed the more friends who smoke a person has, the greater the chance that the person will try cigarettes. Once a person has tried cigarettes, the process of addiction begins. Leventhal and Cleary (1980) have found that trying one cigarette does not generally lead to smoking – a comforting thought since many young people try smoking at least once. Curiously, however, by the fourth cigarette the addictive process is more likely; a person who gets to the fourth cigarette is highly likely to become a smoker.

Research has shown that smokers tend to be from two camps of teenagers: the most and least popular and successful (Mosbach and Leventhal, 1988). People with low self-esteem or high self-esteem, people who are well liked by their peers or those who are not, and those scoring highly on class tests as well as those getting the lowest scores are the most likely to be smokers. Those falling in the middle of these extremes are less likely to smoke. This is shown in Figure 3.2. There is some evidence that smoking can be a form of rebellion among teenagers who are inclined towards it (Jessor and Jessor, 1977). However, this does not explain the fact that parents who smoke are more likely to have children who take up smoking; it is difficult to describe smoking as a rebellious activity when it is also a parental activity.

Study 3.7

AIM Charlton and Blair (1989) wanted to know what factors influenced starting smoking in young boys and girls.

METHOD The researchers surveyed 1213 girls and 1125 boys aged 12–13 years, on their social background, their knowledge of cigarette advertising and the different brands of cigarettes, what they had been taught about smoking and their beliefs about smoking.

RESULTS None of the factors studied significantly predicted smoking in boys, although having a friend who smoked was the factor that had the strongest effect. In girls, however, four of the factors studied predicted smoking uptake; these were smoking by at least one parent, believing that smoking can be a good thing, knowledge of cigarette brands, and having a best friend who was a smoker.

CONCLUSION In female teenagers, smoking can be predicted by whether parents smoke, whether best friends smoke, and by positive views of smoking and knowledge or awareness of cigarette brands available. In boys, these factors do not predict smoking, which suggests that boys smoke for other, unresearched, reasons.

PRACTICAL Activity

In a group of three or four, discuss reasons and explanations for why teenagers who have high self-esteem, are liked by their peers and do well at their studies are likely to take up smoking. Do the same for teenagers who have low self-esteem, are not popular with their peers, and perform poorly at their studies. In what ways are the explanations different for each type of teenager?

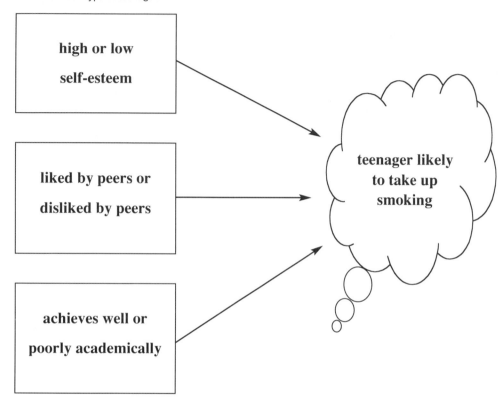

Figure 3.2: Teenagers at one or other extreme are more likely to take up smoking than those in the 'middle ground' (Mosbach and Leventhal, 1988)

Smoking is a habit that is much more prevalent in working-class than middle-class people (General Household Survey, 1999). However, on its own, the social-class factor does not explain smoking behaviour. It is, though, a useful way to demonstrate how various factors can be interlinked. Working-class people tend to have working-class children, and middle-class people middle-class children. As a result, it is not possible to know whether certain people inherit 'addictive personalities' from their parents or whether there is something about social class cultures and upbringing that influence smoking behaviour. However, it is equally likely that the stresses felt by working-class people are dealt with by them by smoking. Although middle-class people experience stress too, the way that they choose to deal with it might be different from the coping mechanisms employed by working-class people. Indeed, since one group is financially better off than the other the ways in which they 'let off steam' may well reflect their disposable incomes. Therefore, while there is a strong social class effect on smoking behaviour, the reasons behind it are far from clear.

Smoking behaviour, paradoxically, can sometimes be seen as an adaptive strategy, intended to reduce psychological stresses and thus as a health-promoting behaviour, although a rather unusual one. Some people smoke to prevent stress, and to help them cope. A perfect example of this view is shown by the work of Graham (1998) who interviewed young women smokers with children, whose main source of income was state benefit. They often argued that they 'needed' a cigarette to help them calm down when the children were crying, or when tempers were raised in the family. By smoking they may intentionally avoid, it is claimed, physical or psychological abuse of their children.

Study 3.8

AIM File, Fluck and Leahy (2001) examined the claim that nicotine has a calming effect, which may be why some people smoke.

METHOD A total of 36 male and female non-smoking students were tested on their ability to perform a cognitive task when given nicotine. Some of the time they received nicotine, sometimes not. Neither the students nor the researchers knew if the participants were being given nicotine or a 'dummy' drug.

RESULTS In the non-smoking sample, nicotine did not increase attention or memory. It made the male participants more aggressive and anxious, but actually calmed down the females taking part.

CONCLUSION The researchers concluded that women may take up smoking because it can have the effect of reducing anxiety and stress, so that campaigns to prevent people taking up smoking should concentrate on offering people ways to combat stress so that they do not try smoking cigarettes to calm them down.

Work on the reasons why people smoke has uncovered some obvious answers and some less obvious. Some people simply claim that they like the taste of tobacco smoke, or the smell, or some other sensual property of the process of smoking (Leventhal and Avis, 1976). Leventhal and Avis also noted that smokers' self-reports of smoking behaviour centre around habit, addiction, or the properties of a cigarette to make a person feel more alert and attentive or to reduce anxiety and produce a sense of calm. Smokers often feel the need to smoke with a drink of alcohol or after a meal (Pomerleau and Pomerleau, 1989), something difficult to explain

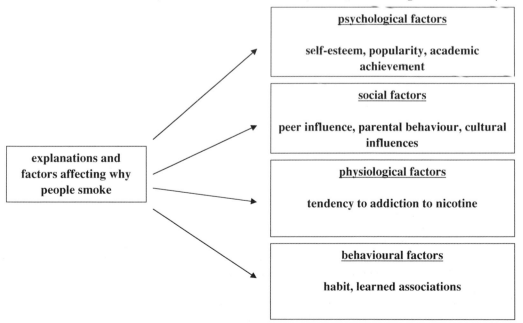

Figure 3.3: The main factors influencing and explaining why people smoke

easily but worrying since if eating and smoking are somehow paired up there is a distinct encouragement to smoke every time a person eats. Figure 3.3 summarises the main explanations for smoking that we have considered here.

EVALUATIVE COMMENT

The pairing up of smoking episodes with other events leads us now to briefly consider one of the views of why it is so difficult to stop smoking. That is, the effects of stimulus–response association, or conditioning. Common stimulus–response pairings in everyday life could include:

- **hunger = eat food**

- **sound of breaking glass = look out!**

- **red traffic light = stop**

- **leave the house = close the front door**

- **nearing house = reach for keys.**

People may smoke because they learn to pair up the act of having a cigarette with its effects, or with some other act or event. Smoking can increase alertness. If a person desires being alert, and a cigarette provides this, a stimulus–response association is immediately set up. If a person associates smoking with being with friends and having fun, not only might they smoke when among friends, but also when alone and/or not having fun, in order to generate a similar feeling.

GIVING UP SMOKING

When psychologists deal with smoking by helping people to give up the habit, they sometimes do so by using behavioural techniques involving conditioning. **Aversion therapy** (Kent and Dalgleish, 1996) is a form of this. In aversion therapy, an attempt is made to deter someone from smoking by getting them to concentrate on the negative aspects of it. Aversion therapy can come in weak or strong forms. A weak form would be allowing someone to smoke but expecting them to focus on unpleasant aspects of smoking, such as the burning smoke and its taste, while they do so. A stronger form would be forcing the smoker to

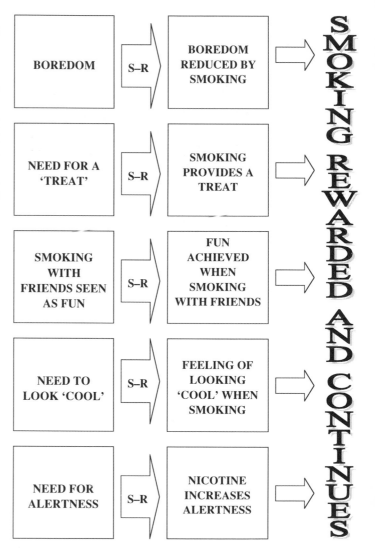

Figure 3.4: Behaviourist explanation of why people continue to smoke; stimulus-response links are set up when the person has needs that can be met by smoking

smoke more than usual until they feel ill from it, known as **rapid smoking**. Repeated episodes of this 'over-smoking' can deter the individual from smoking permanently. Such drastic methods are rarely used any more since they are theoretically quite dangerous.

Study 3.9

AIM Houtsmuller and Stitzer (1999) investigated whether cravings for cigarettes could be reduced by episodes of rapid smoking.

METHOD A total of 14 participants aged between 18 and 50 took part in three sessions involving either rapid smoking, normal smoking or no smoking. Their cravings were recorded over the next three hours.

RESULTS Rapid smoking reduced cravings compared with normal smoking or a period of abstinence from smoking. However, later smoking behaviour (once the three-hour session was over) was not changed by rapid smoking.

CONCLUSION The authors concluded that rapid smoking can reduce cravings, but that cravings do not predict smoking behaviour some hours after rapid smoking has ceased.

Images like this can be used to make people think twice about their habit

Conditioning is not the only way health psychologists have of helping people stop smoking, although there is often some element of conditioning, whether covert or overt, in many of the techniques that are used. The most basic form of anti-smoking technique is the health promotion campaign, aimed at groups rather than individuals. By warning people about the dangers of smoking, it is hoped that people will turn away from it. Indeed, there is evidence that such campaigns do work.

Egger *et al.* (1983) report the success of a three-year Australian media campaign in coastal New South Wales. The campaign had a threefold purpose: to stop people smoking, to get them to cut down on fat in their diets and to get them to participate in regular exercise. The media campaign was extensive, involving radio and television advertisements, newspaper articles, T-shirts, stickers and self-help kits. Two towns were enrolled, and one other served as a control town, where no such campaign was run. In one town the media programme ran alone, and in the other the media programme ran with a community-based intervention scheme. In the joint programme, the best success was reported for young men (aged 18–25), for whom there was a decrease in smoking rates of 15.7 per cent. The worst was for older women (over 65), for whom the figure was 6.1 per cent. However, in the control town there was a decrease of as much as 5.1 per cent over the course of the study, for women aged 18–25 and men aged 36–55. Therefore, we must subtract the appropriate control decreases from the decreases observed from the towns enrolled in the media campaign. Doing this shows real declines in smoking rates of about 12 per cent for men aged 18–25 and 4 per cent for women over 65. A reduction of around 12 per cent in smoking rates in young men could have considerable benefits in terms of savings of lives and resources in later years. What is clear from this Australian study is that the absence of a campaign is worse than running a media campaign, and that running a community programme alongside a media campaign reduces smoking most successfully.

EVALUATIVE COMMENT

This study lacked a useful comparison group. There was not a town enrolled in the study that received a community programme but no media campaign. As a result, there is no way of knowing if the media-and-community group owed its success to the community intervention rather than the media campaign. The researchers, to be more conclusive, should have included such a comparison town in the study.

Pressure can be put on smokers by governments placing a high tax on tobacco products, thus increasing their cost to the consumer. While this might not prove to be a particularly strong deterrent for adults with good incomes, it might put off younger people. Anti-smoking campaigns often try to frighten people away from smoking by associating smoking with its dangers. Taxing tobacco products makes smoking more of an unpleasant activity because it takes a large amount of a person's disposal income.

EVALUATIVE COMMENT

Generally, combined programmes work better than single techniques, and are more likely to last. One of the first steps in getting someone to give up smoking may involve a substitute way of introducing nicotine into the blood, without having to smoke tobacco. Nicotine patches and gum are a controlled way of doing this that have attracted much attention in recent years. There is substantial evidence that they can make a difference. An analysis of 17 placebo-controlled studies into nicotine patches was conducted by Fiore *et al.* (1994). On average, 9 per cent of people wearing a placebo patch (containing no nicotine) gave up smoking, whereas 22 per cent of those with the genuine nicotine patch did. No one knew which type of patch they were wearing.

PRACTICAL Activity

Most of us know people who have stopped smoking. Get together with the rest of your class, and each of you identify people that you know who successfully gave up smoking. Ask what methods they used to do so. Then make one large list, and see which methods turned out to be the most successful and which the least.

Study 3.10

AIM Gourlay *et al.* (1994) carried out a study to determine which factors were most important in the outcome of using nicotine patches to help people to stop smoking.

METHOD They surveyed 1481 people, who smoked at least 15 cigarettes per day, about their smoking habits and attempts to give up.

RESULTS Over the six months of the data-collection period, 316 of the participants stopped smoking. The most successful participants (in terms of quit rates) were men, people over 40, those married or living with a partner, those having high motivation to succeed, and people who expressed concern over gaining weight after giving up.

CONCLUSION People who smoked marijuana were less likely to succeed in giving up (hardly surprising since the drug is often mixed with tobacco, and that some people continued to use marijuana when enrolled in the smoking-cessation study). The most unusual finding was that people concerned about gaining weight were *more* likely, rather than less, to quit successfully. Weight-gain concerns are normally expected to deter people from stopping smoking.

EVALUATIVE COMMENT

Allowing people access to nicotine via patches assists with the physical aspects of nicotine addiction, but does not deal with the more psychosocial aspects, for example the environmental cues to smoke such as stress, drinking coffee and pressure from friends who smoke. These require other approaches. A combination of techniques, such as nicotine patches, a self-help strategy and some other intervention by a therapist or doctor, is the most likely to work (Lando, 1977).

Alcohol

Alcohol is a legal drug that causes serious health and social problems. Excessive consumption can lead to liver disease, heart disease, mental degeneration and cancers of the digestive tract. Alcohol is implicated in many violent acts against the person, and is also associated with reduced sexual functioning. It is claimed to be involved in 60 per cent of suicide attempts, 30 per cent of divorces and 20 per cent of admissions to psychiatric hospital (Bennett, 2000).

It does not require much experience of the world to know that alcohol affects behaviour, and is a psychoactive substance. It depresses the action of the nervous system. People under the influence of alcohol speak more slowly and less well, they are less able to walk or perform motor and co-ordinated hand movements, and their reaction times are slowed considerably. Alcohol lowers psychological inhibitions, with the consequence that people who are drunk may do and say things they would not normally do and say, and embarrass themselves. People may take more risks when under the influence of alcohol, and are much more likely to injure themselves. Large quantities of alcohol are bad for the body: the next day people often report a 'hangover'. This consists of headaches, nausea, even tremors. This occurs because the body has, effectively, been poisoned. So why do some people regularly do this to themselves?

Like smoking, alcohol is something that often appeals to younger people. Studies show that people usually have their first experiences with alcohol as teenagers, and, often, before they are legally allowed to buy and drink it. In this sense, alcohol use reflects trends in smoking behaviour. In Britain, in an effort to prevent alcohol being made to look appealing to children,

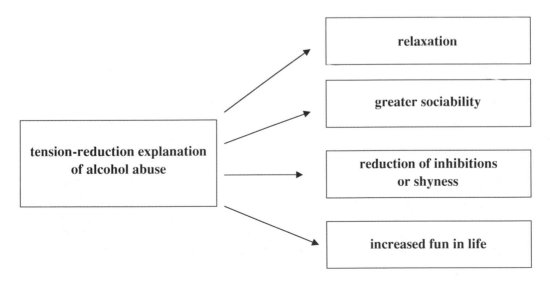

Figure 3.5: Key factors underlying the tension-reduction hypothesis of alcohol abuse, proposed by Cappel and Greeley (1987)

it is the law that advertising for alcohol products must not show people who *look* under the age of 18, even if they are older.

Drinking alcohol to excess is something that is found across the world, certain countries excepted, and there are regional trends in alcohol consumption and abuse. In Europe, French people, for example, drink a great deal of alcohol. As a result, deaths from cirrhosis of the liver are very common in France (Schmidt, 1977). Health problems related to alcohol will vary from country to country. When reading what follows, remember that the vast majority of research into alcohol abuse has been conducted in the western world, principally in North America, Britain and parts of Europe. What motivates a drinker in Scotland does not necessarily motivate one in Chile. As Napoleon (1999) explains, alcoholism among the Yup'ik Inuit people of Alaska may be a disease stemming from spiritual (psychological) upset due to the political and financial weakness of their people. It is unlikely that a health psychologist in Britain would, or could, make such a claim about English problem drinkers. In well-researched populations, alcoholism develops partly as a response to forms of stress, known as the **tension-reduction hypothesis** (Cappell and Greeley, 1987). This is shown in Figure 3.5. People report needing a drink to relax, or to make them more sociable. Some people like the fact that alcohol lowers their inhibitions, allowing them to 'let their hair down' and join in the fun. Alcohol does tend to work, and so further states of tension are treated with more alcohol.

Typically, problem drinking comes in two main forms: binge drinking and chronic alcoholism. The binge drinker may not be physically addicted to alcohol, but will regularly drink large amounts of alcohol during a night out. The chronic alcoholic is addicted to alcohol and may spend little or none of their waking life sober. What follows is concerned with chronic alcoholism; binge drinking has been much less extensively researched.

INTERVENING IN ALCOHOL ABUSE

There are a number of ways in which alcohol abuse can be tackled – ranging from governmental strategies such as taxation and health-promotion campaigns, to individual treatment programmes developed by health psychologists. The individual treatment programmes closely match those used with smokers.

Before an alcoholic can be treated, it is often necessary to engage in *detoxification*; this is often referred to as 'drying out'. The individual is denied all access to alcohol for a period of time, and until all traces of alcohol are out of the body and the symptoms of alcohol withdrawal (like tremors, hallucinations and nausea) have ceased. Only then is the process of overcoming the psychological dependence likely to be successful. Hence this may be seen as a two-stage process, as shown in Figure 3.6.

Various behavioural techniques using conditioning have been successful. These may involve taking a substance – such as 'emetine' (technically known as an antidypsotropic medication) –

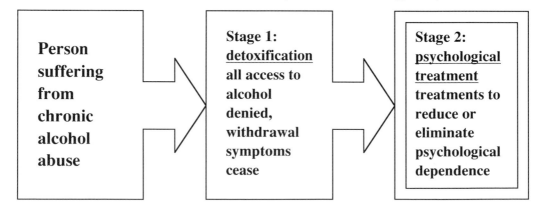

Figure 3.6: Two-stage process for treating people who abuse alcohol

that causes the person to vomit if they then drink alcohol. A typical alcohol aversion therapy would involve having regular alcoholic drinks after taking emetine by injection, and then the person would be sick after each drink. The aim is to make the person associate alcoholic drinks with bouts of vomiting, thus making them ill-disposed to taking further alcohol. Wiens and Menustik (1983) reported that over half of their patients stayed away from alcohol in the two years after the therapy. Another, more modern and less extreme version of emetic therapy involves giving people a drug like emetine and simply explaining to them what is likely to happen if they drink alcohol. The aim here is to prevent any alcohol being consumed. This is not the same as normal aversion therapy, however, since the aim is not to associate alcohol with something bad by direct pairing up, but simply to scare the individual away from alcohol based on a 'stay away from it or else' view.

Study 3.11

AIM Wiens and Menustik (1983) investigated the success of an aversion-therapy routine for alcoholic patients.

METHOD The researchers conducted a one- and three-year follow-up study of 685 alcoholic patients involved in a programme of alcohol aversion using conditioning. Patients took a drug that made them sick every time they drank alcohol. The participants were all enrolled in a two-week long programme of treatment followed by occasional sessions after this to reinforce the effects of the treatment.

RESULTS Of the patients enrolled in the study, 63 per cent said that they had stayed away from alcohol for a year after the treatment was over, and 31 per cent remained drink-free after three years.

CONCLUSION Aversion therapy involving drugs that make alcohol intolerable to the body can have substantial effects in reducing rates of alcoholism.

One rather famous and different way of dealing with alcoholism is that taken by Alcoholics Anonymous (AA). Here, people meet to deal with their drinking behaviour by sharing their experiences and admitting to each other that they have made mistakes by becoming addicted to alcohol. The AA method relies on a social support mechanism, something psychologists know can heavily influence health behaviour (Ogden, 2000). New members talk to longer-standing members about their experiences, and successful ways of staying sober and free from alcohol are shared. Unlike many programmes established by psychologists and other health professionals, AA does not believe in moderation as a key to controlling alcoholism; it argues that total abstinence is the only reliable way to stop people abusing alcohol. Its rather 'confessional' approach seems to work for some people, although studies directly comparing this method with others are few and far between.

EVALUATIVE COMMENT

Alcohol misuse is a good example of the nature of human behaviour in general. People do things for many reasons, and there are probably as many approaches to solving problems as there are reasons for the problems developing in the first place. Alcohol misuse is similar to smoking in that parental and peer pressure can obviously play a large part, as can the need to relax and 'let one's hair down'. However, alcohol differs from smoking in that a small amount of alcohol can be argued to be beneficial to health. Most doctors agree that small amounts of alcohol, especially red wine, can help to reduce rates of heart disease. No doctor would tell you that the occasional cigarette is good for you. Both things are addictive, however, and so a small amount of alcohol can lead to drinking more and more until a problem develops. Balancing healthy alcohol use against excessive and damaging misuse is difficult, and many people do this naturally. Some others, however, cannot. One potential area for further research

in health psychology might be in identifying those people who are at risk from addiction to alcohol and who should, therefore, avoid it altogether.

Since alcohol forms a very valuable coping mechanism for many people, programmes designed to wean people off alcohol need to help the individual to find other means of coping, otherwise the programmes are likely to fail. Approaches based on this ethos try to replace alcohol with a new set of coping skills. These include the social skills necessary to refuse alcohol when it is offered, and to avoid situations that tempt the individual or bring about cravings for alcohol. The whole programme is often framed with some kind of 'punishment' should it fail; this is known as **contingency contracting** (a contract based upon a contingency, i.e. a particular outcome). Here the therapist and patient enter into a contract with each other (Edelmann, 2000). There is a financial or other loss associated with failing to meet the demands of the programme. Therefore, there is a practical incentive for the person to keep in line with expectations. For those people who object to 'punishment' in these situations, one can just as easily imagine a *reward* for sticking to the programme, such as being given one's money back at the end. As is the case with giving up smoking, these combined therapies are more likely to work than any single technique used in isolation. The success of behavioural approaches that include skills training is good, as demonstrated by Longabaugh and Morgenstern (1999) in a review of the evidence. They conclude that although the approach is not better than others when used in isolation, it is beneficial when used in conjunction with other therapies, such as treatment using general social skills training, self-help group activities and chemical therapies.

Study 3.12

AIM Litt *et al.* (2003) wanted to test out a cognitive–behavioural programme involving coping skills training versus a therapy involving discussing personal relationships, with the aim of finding out which was best in helping people who misused alcohol.

METHOD The study involved 128 men and women who were dependent upon alcohol. They received 26 weeks of treatment either involving coping skills training or an interactive therapy aimed at working through interpersonal relationships and identifying areas of social life that might be problematic for a person who misuses alcohol.

RESULTS Coping skills and alcohol drinking behaviour were examined both before the treatment and as much as 18 months after the treatment started. Both treatment types reduced alcohol misuse equally, and both types improved coping skills. Successful development of coping skills was related to alcohol misuse, regardless of the treatment programme involved.

CONCLUSION The researchers concluded that coping skills training is not needed as a specialist programme of therapy. Any therapy that can promote good coping skills can be useful.

EVALUATIVE COMMENT

Litt *et al.*'s (2003) study shows that coping is an essential part of dealing with alcohol misuse. If a person has the skills and strategies to cope with their problem, then they are quite likely to recover from alcoholism. What is important is that it does not matter where these coping skills come from. Many types of treatment might help to increase coping, not just those aimed directly at providing those skills. Therefore, in the future health psychologists should, perhaps, find out which techniques are best at promoting coping, and cease using those therapies that do not increase coping.

Sexual health

Sexual behaviour and sexual practices may be healthy or unhealthy for the individual. Sexual activity can be important to the individual in maintaining mental and physical health. Like any exercise, in moderation the body welcomes it. Mental well-being can be enhanced by sexual activity because it is often about feeling wanted and accepted by others. However, it can also be detrimental to the mind and body. Sexually transmitted disease (STD) can and does kill people, and injures many more (including making them sterile), and unwanted sexual experiences (either unwanted at the time, such as rape or abuse, or on reflection giving rise to later feelings of regret or shame) can cause significant stress and trauma for the individual.

SEXUALLY TRANSMITTED DISEASES

Sexually transmitted diseases (STDs) show changes in their prevalence over time in populations. However, rarely does any single STD disappear from a population, meaning that all sexual encounters carry a risk of contracting an STD. Sexually transmitted diseases include HIV/AIDS (dealt with separately below), syphilis, herpes and gonorrhoea. Much of the research conducted in health psychology has focused on STD in relation to condom use by men, since condoms can protect against many STDs. This, however, overlooks STD transmission between women, for instance, for whom condoms are not applicable.

Health psychologists construct theories and models to understand why people think and behave the way that they do, and what influences their decisions to protect their sexual health or to take risks. Any model relying upon 'thought' as a factor may fall short of explaining behaviour, since, as Abraham and Sheeran (1994) suggest, people are usually aroused when engaging in sexual acts, and so are less likely to think clearly about what they are doing. Sexual arousal may break the link between what a person, when not aroused, thinks they would do and what they actually do when aroused.

All around the world, authorities use a range of techniques to educate people and change their behaviour

AIDS is not always an STD, but it can be. Drug users who inject, people who have received blood and blood products such as plasma, and foetuses, can become infected with the HIV virus; sexual activity is not a part of this method of transmission. The human immunodeficiency virus (HIV) transmits itself largely through contact between blood, vaginal mucus and semen, in any combination. The presence of wounds in the mouth, on the genitals, and so on, can increase its likelihood of transmission, especially sexually. In many countries, in Africa in particular, HIV infection is widespread (with around 80 per cent of the world's HIV-infected people living in Africa). Poverty, poor nutrition, lack of education about sexual health, high rates of prostitution (linked to poverty), and lack of medical resources can be seen as the primary causes. If people cannot afford condoms and have not been told how HIV infection occurs, it is not surprising that the rates of transmission are high. In places where prostitution is one of a very small number of ways in which women (and men) can make money to clothe, feed and protect their families, the HIV virus is more likely to spread. Recent research has identified, however, a group of women prostitutes in one African community who appear to be immune to HIV infection (Fine, 2000). Doctors are now looking at ways of replicating this immunity in order to develop some kind of inoculation.

AIM Oakeshott *et al.* (2000) conducted a study to look at the success of promoting condom use in women attending GP practices.

METHOD The study involved 1382 women aged from 16–34, and 28 GP practices in South London were involved in the study. When the women were attending their doctors' surgeries in order to have their routine smear tests, a random half of them were specifically given information about sexually transmitted diseases and were given condoms. Those in the other half of the sample were simply surveyed after they had seen their doctor to see if their doctors had mentioned STDs and had given them condoms.

RESULTS Although more women in the condom-promotion groups were given information about STDs and more were given condoms, there was no difference later in actual condom use.

CONCLUSION Giving out condoms and providing information about STDs that can be prevented by condom use does not necessarily increase condom use in sexually active women. This may be because there are other factors that may influence condom use in women, such as their male partners' opinions about condom use.

PRACTICAL Activity

Conduct an Internet search to find out about a sexual health promotion campaign of your choice. Alternatively, visit a local clinic or health centre to pick up a leaflet about sexual health. In a group of three or four, discuss the content of the campaign or leaflet and list the reasons why you think it might work and the reasons why it might not. Make sure you consider not just the campaign content itself but also where and when it is made available to people.

One of the ways in which health promotion campaigns work is by frightening people into engaging in health-protective behaviours. So-called 'scare tactics' are increasingly common, and are often used in campaigns against drink-driving, with real footage from accidents and real victims or perpetrators telling their stories. One such campaign was run in Australia in the 1980s, involving images of the 'grim reaper' to publicise AIDS and create anxiety such that people would protect themselves (Rigby *et al.*, 1989). It did not work. While the campaign did increase awareness and knowledge, it did not have an effect on behaviour. Scaring people, or *trying* to do so, can have the opposite effect. Examples of the type of thinking that a scare tactic might engender are shown in Figure 3.7.

Denial is a particularly strong phenomenon at times. Temoshok *et al.* (1987) asked people in various US cities if AIDS was a health concern for them specifically. People in New York were most concerned by AIDS, with 52 per cent of people admitting that it was a health concern for them; people in San Francisco were the least concerned in the cities studied, with a figure of 33 per cent 'yes' responses. There are, proportionally, more people in San Francisco who are HIV-positive than anywhere else in America. Of course, this does not mean that denial is the only explanation. In a city familiar with AIDS, knowledge levels about it are likely to be high, and, if behaviour follows knowledge, people in San Francisco might have perceived themselves to be relatively safe from AIDS because they know how to protect themselves from HIV as best as possible. This is a reasonable explanation since Temoshok *et al.*'s study also compared attitudes of people with different sexual orientations. Gay, straight and bisexual men were surveyed. AIDS was perceived by the gay and bisexual men as a bigger problem; they also had more knowledge about it and reported a greater perceived susceptibility to it. However, perceived risk was not accompanied by changes in sexual behaviour – perhaps again reinforcing the 'denial explanation' of these results.

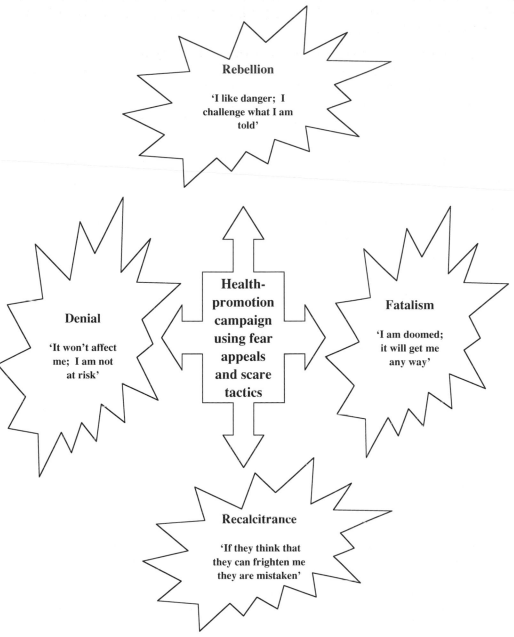

Figure 3.7: Unwanted psychological effects of 'scare campaigns', resulting in little effect on changing behaviour

PRACTICAL Activity

Think about the threats to sexual health. Work in a group to invent a campaign to try to promote sexual health. Think of using all available media, such as television/radio, magazine advertisements and posters. Do you think that it would be a good or a bad thing if every person with a mobile phone received a text message saying 'Think Protective Sex'?

Scare tactics are particularly unlikely to work in isolation. Telling someone to do something or else risk death may be a good way to get across the seriousness of a situation, but does not provide them with any tools for the job. Someone may accept the message that condoms should be worn to reduce the risk of HIV infection, but may not know how to fit them or, more commonly perhaps, may lack the social skills needed to raise the issue of condoms with a partner. The fear of AIDS can actually be supplanted by a fear of doing the wrong thing in an intimate situation or feeling silly by making a nervous attempt to discuss protection.

In addition, everyone is not equally assertive. Therefore, skills training and education are important. In Britain, initial scare campaigns with sombre images were followed up by TV advertisements where scenarios involving heterosexual couples were played out, showing that it does not have to be embarrassing or off-putting to talk about and use condoms, or that it is often advisable to avoid penetrative sex if condoms are not available. Thus, the aim is that people are frightened about the prospect of AIDS but are also vicariously able to learn about how to deal with intimate situations involving safer sex.

EVALUATIVE COMMENT

Getting individuals to change their behaviour to reduce the risk of ending up HIV-positive tends to centre around four main strands. As Stein (1990) points out these are:

- **using condoms**
- **selecting partners more carefully**
- **limiting numbers of partners**
- **limiting type of sexual activity.**

These may be easier to intend than to carry out. Again, appropriate education is necessary. From a point of view of relative ignorance, a person may not understand enough about condoms to use them. In some countries, condoms are expensive, and outside of the budget of poorer sectors of society. Some people might not know how to select partners. For example, if they do not have a good knowledge of AIDS, they might not know that avoiding sexual intercourse with people who inject drugs is sensible. Similarly, limiting partners may not be an option for a person who is living in a peer group for whom 'promiscuity' is the norm. Finally, limiting type of sexual activity can be difficult. Not only does this require that a person knows which activities are in the safer-sex category and which not, but it also implies that people have choice in what they do. A person who is forced to comply with another's sexual requirements may not have the freedom to limit sex to non-penetrative acts and 'safer sex'. Equally, some HIV infection is likely to occur through partners who have trusted their lovers to be monogamous when in fact they have not been. Marks *et al.* (1991) demonstrated that 52 per cent of men who were HIV-positive did not tell their sexual partners about this. Control, and informed choice, therefore, are not always the appropriate terms to use in describing sexual behaviour and intentions.

3.3 Theories of lifestyle change

What people think about their health, and how they perceive illness (both generally and their own), is fundamental to health psychology. If we know why people do something, we can work with them to alter their behaviour. Much research in health psychology is focused on creating theories that explain people's behaviours in respect to protecting their health.

The health belief model (HBM)

Possibly the most important body of work in this area, certainly historically, is the study around the **health belief model**. This dates back to Rosenstock (1966), and has frequently been used as

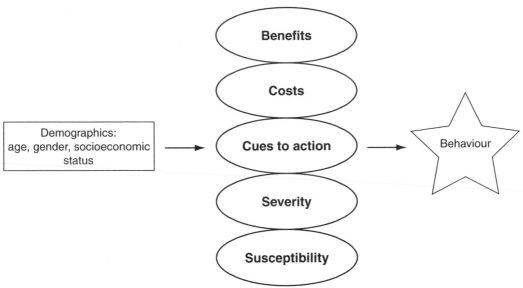

Figure 3.8: The early health belief model (Forshaw, 2002b)

a framework for understanding **health beliefs** since then. The HBM is based around five themes, as shown in Figure 3.8.

To predict the likelihood that a person will engage in a particular health behaviour in response to a specific health threat (like a potential illness or disease), the HBM requires that we consider what the person *perceives* as the costs and benefits of engaging in the health behaviour (sometimes called barriers and benefits), what they *perceive* as the severity of the threat, what they *perceive* as their personal susceptibility to the threat, and any cues to action that exist or occur, which can come from inside the individual or outside of them. (A cue to action is something that acts as a prompt to the person to do something to protect their health. It might be a symptom or sign in their body, or it might come in the form of advice from a doctor or a friend.)

The health belief model is a rational model, which means that it is based on the idea that people think their behaviours through before engaging in them. The costs and benefits are weighed against each other, and it is hoped that the benefits of a behaviour will outweigh the costs. In order for someone to do something like giving up smoking, they have to believe that the 'bad' side of smoking is more important than what they see as the 'good' side. So, they will weigh up the pleasures they get from continuing to smoke cigarettes, such as relaxation, against the costs such as breathlessness, lung cancer and having less money. They will also assess the severity of the health threat posed by smoking. So they will think about the likely health consequences of continuing smoking. Furthermore, they will do this by thinking about the effects of smoking on *them*, personally. They might believe that they are in a low-risk group, or alternatively that they are in a high-risk group, and they are more likely to give up smoking if they perceive the threat of lung cancer (for example). They might think about their age, because smoking is more likely to create health problems in an older person than a younger one. Smoking is also particularly bad for people who are unfit and overweight, and who eat fatty foods. They might also take into account any smokers they know who have suffered from ill-health or died because of smoking. Finally, cues to action will play a part in their decision to either continue smoking or to give up. If they do not feel that smoking is causing them any problems, they may continue to smoke. However, if they are experiencing breathlessness, or if they have been told to give up by friends and family or a doctor, these cues might tip the balance in favour of giving up.

Note that, in the health belief model, perceptions are all-important. The real threat a person faces does not really matter at all. People act on perceived threats. If a person happens to know the facts and statistics about a disease, then their perceived threat might match very closely the actual threat. There is one other principle to be considered, which was included in later formulations of the model (Becker *et al.*, 1977). This is *health motivation*. This is a way of describing a person's interest in health matters, and the extent to which they are generally motivated to act on the issue of health. Some people don't really want to be fit and healthy, whereas for others this is important.

We now can turn to research on the HBM, here investigating adolescent condom use in Scotland, as reported by Sheeran and Abraham (1995).

Study 3.14

AIM Sheeran and Abraham (1995) investigated whether the HBM could explain condom use in adolescents.

METHOD Two sets of adolescents were identified, those at 16 and those at 18 years of age. An HBM-based questionnaire was sent out, yielding 690 returns, and it was sent out again a year later. Pairing up the questionnaires, the researchers ended up with 333 responses they could use. Questions included those about intended condom use.

RESULTS The results were not encouraging, in that HBM components did not predict condom use (and thus HIV-preventative behaviour).

CONCLUSION The authors suggested that it might be the case that safer-sex health beliefs are essentially in place for all participants, but that other factors lead to actual health behaviour. However, the results were complicated by a gender difference in the relationship between intention and behaviour. For males, there was a small but significant relationship between the two, but for women there was not. Therefore, some of the ideas in the HBM did predict condom use in males, but not in females. It might be that females rely more on males in relation to condom use, because they see it as a men's issue.

EVALUATIVE COMMENT

The authors argue that this might reflect the lack of choice women may feel they have in sexual relationships. If a man chooses to wear a condom he might find it easy to translate this choice into action, whereas, prior to the creation of the female condom, a woman had to rely on a man to use this contraceptive device. This shows that the HBM, while a good starting point for health psychologists, misses out many factors that determine behaviour. For this reason, other models have since taken precedence.

PRACTICAL Activity

Interview a friend to see if the factors in the health belief model seem to work together in respect of a health behaviour. Therefore, you will first need to construct some questions that match the aspects of the model. For example, if you are interviewing someone on how they gave up smoking, you would need a question on cues to action, which might be something like 'Did anyone say anything to you which helped you to give up?'

The theory of planned behaviour

Like many health psychology models, the **theory of planned behaviour (TPB)** developed from work in social psychology, specifically the theory of reasoned action. Ajzen (1985; 1988; 1991) suggested that perceived behavioural control affects intentions, and that intentions then influence actual behaviour. *Perceived behavioural control* works in conjunction with two other factors, which are *subjective norms* and *attitudes to behaviour* (see Figure 3.9). Let us consider what each of these terms might mean.

Perceived behavioural control is the extent to which a person perceives that they are in control of their behaviour and are thus going to be able to achieve a desired health behaviour, such as eating more carbohydrate/less fat, or exercising. This is a belief based not only on psychological factors such as personality and ability, but external factors such as personal finances.

Subjective norms are beliefs about the desirability of carrying out a certain health behaviour in the society, social group and culture in which the person lives. Attitudes to behaviour are views that people hold. Every person will have attitudes towards performing a certain behaviour, either good or bad, strong or weak, and attitudes towards the end result or outcome of that behaviour. Whether or not someone genuinely intends to perform a behaviour will depend on a combination of what society tells them about that behaviour, what they feel they are capable of doing, and what their attitudes to that behaviour and the potential result of it will be. A person addicted to heroin might have strong beliefs that heroin addiction is not socially acceptable, especially if their friends and family are disapproving (subjective norms). They may then have a positive attitude to shrugging off the addiction, and the outcome of doing so, such as becoming a normal citizen again and acquiring work (attitudes to behaviour). However, they might not have much belief that they are capable of giving up the drug, especially since it is highly addictive psychologically (perceived behavioural control). As a consequence, their intention to give up heroin might be low, so they are not likely to engage in that behaviour.

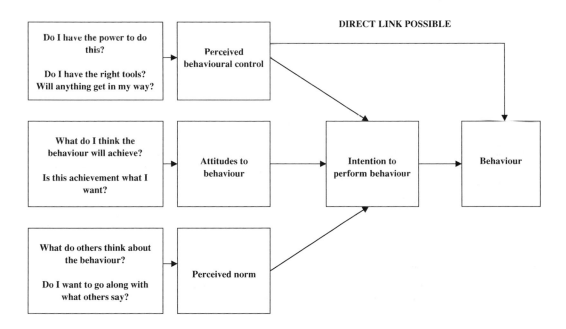

Figure 3.9: The components of the theory of planned behaviour

Study 3.15

AIM An early test of the theory of planned behaviour in health came through research conducted by Schifter and Ajzen (1985), which looked at weight loss in female students.

METHOD Students were enrolled in the study to lose weight over a period of six weeks. At the beginning of the study their attitudes to weight loss were probed, as were their opinions about dieting norms, intentions as to losing weight, and their perceived ability to manage their weight loss.

RESULTS Intention to lose weight was significantly predicted by subjective norms, attitudes and perceived control.

CONCLUSION Young women who want to lose weight are most likely to succeed if they believe they are capable of doing so.

EVALUATIVE COMMENT

In Schifter and Ajzen's (1985) study, intention to lose weight and perceived control did predict some of the actual weight loss, but not as much as the researchers might have liked. The most interesting finding, it might be argued, was that intention to lose weight predicted weight loss only in those people with higher perceived behavioural control. In other words, the women who intended to lose weight but did not think they would manage to eat fewer calories every day for six weeks were able to lose much less weight compared with those women who had the intention *and* believed they were capable of eating less. In common-sense terms, the best of intentions are not enough if a person does not really believe in themselves and their ability to carry out those intentions.

Self-efficacy theory

A number of theorists suggest that perceived self-efficacy (the belief that a person holds about being able to perform a certain behaviour) is a primary determinant of health behaviour (e.g. Schwarzer, 1992). This is remarkably close to what the TPB is based on: an idea of perceived control affecting behaviour. Schwarzer's work is often called the **health action process approach (HAPA)**. The emphasis on a process is highly significant; in this model the person moves from one set of plans and cognitions to another in their decision-making process, which, ideally, leads to an intention to act and then measurable behaviour. Before people can act, they have to be motivated to act. The motivation phase of this model involves the person's perceived self-efficacy (if they believe they are able to act and act well), their assessment of the health threat (how severe the threat is and how vulnerable to it they are), and their outcome expectancies (what they think will happen if they do act).

Provided that people have a high degree of perceived self-efficacy, view the outcome of the health behaviour to be beneficial, and see the threat of the illness or disease as sufficiently strong, they will then act. In the second phase (often referred to as the volitional stage), people must think positively and constructively about the health behaviour and how to achieve it (cognitive factors that can be termed 'action plans') and they must have appropriate social support and finances (situational or environmental factors). Self-efficacy permeates this volitional phase, too, since action plans are bound to be based on what the person realistically thinks they can do. There is no use setting goals that you have no confidence in yourself to achieve.

An example of self-efficacy theory in relation to health could be when a person wants to take up regular exercise. Before the behaviour, such as going to the gym, can begin, the person must want to do it. They must have the motivation. Their motivation might be affected by how much they believe they are able to stick to a schedule of fitting in visits to the gym with the rest of their life, and how much they believe that it will do them good. In addition, they will think about what will happen to them if they do not bother with this behaviour. That is, how much they think that being fit and healthy will keep disease and illness at bay. In the next stage, they will set out plans for achieving this behaviour. This might include working out how to afford gym membership costs, and finding time in their diary for regular trips to the gym. If they have support from friends or family, this will help. For instance, a person may have a small child that needs to be looked after. If someone offers to baby-sit for them, this will be very useful support. Without it, it might be impossible for them to get fit, even if they want to. When they are satisfied that they are able to get fit, that they really want to and that their finances will allow it, the behaviour can begin.

Study 3.16

AIM Povey *et al.* (2000) investigated the theory of planned behaviour in dietary behaviours, but with reference to the additional factors of perceived control and self-efficacy.

METHOD They asked their participants questions about behaviour and intentions towards eating a low-fat diet and eating five portions of fruit and vegetables daily. Part of the purpose of the study was to identify whether perceived behavioural control (PBC) and self-efficacy are separate concepts, since some have argued that they are one and the same thing. Povey *et al.* suggest that they are different, and that PBC refers to whether a person believes they can make a difference to their own behaviour and that self-efficacy is specifically related to how difficult the person perceives the proposed health behaviour to be.

RESULTS They found that both factors predicted intentions to have a low-fat diet and eat fruit and vegetables, but that the stronger predictor of the two was self-efficacy.

CONCLUSION They argue that a person's intentions to perform a behaviour are affected more by how difficult they think that behaviour would be to engage in, rather than how much they think they would be in control of their behaviour. While the authors use these findings to support the TPB, there is also evidence here that self-efficacy theory has its place.

Bray *et al.* (2001) looked at self-efficacy in relation to attendance at exercise classes. However, they also investigated the role of what is called *proxy efficacy*. This leads on from the issue of proxy control, which is basically handing over some or all of the control over a certain issue to another person. Most democratic countries work this way, in that once we have elected a particular government, we expect them to deal with issues on our behalf. Proxy efficacy, therefore, is the extent to which we believe that a person has the skills and abilities required to assist us or carry out duties on our behalf. In the case of exercise classes, the proxy in question is the fitness instructor who leads the classes. In a study over a number of weeks, Bray *et al.* (2001) researched 127 women who were attending fitness classes. They found that there was a small but significant relationship between proxy efficacy and self-efficacy. Therefore, the extent to which someone believes that a powerful other (the instructor) is capable and efficient relates to the extent to which they believe that they can overcome barriers to their own success in a health behaviour context. Looking at attendance, the researchers split the women into experienced exercisers and novices. Self-efficacy and proxy efficacy predicted attendance moderately in the novices, but there was no observed prediction in the experienced exercisers. What this tells us is that when people are starting to take up exercise, a good instructor can 'make or break' their success. Of course, in terms of self-efficacy theory, this study shows us that not only does self-efficacy influence health behaviours, but that proxy efficacy, where appropriate, must also be taken into account. In addition, the contribution of these factors to the performance of health behaviour depends on the experience of the person.

PRACTICAL Activity

Choose three health behaviours, such as eating more fresh fruit and vegetables, going jogging or using condoms. Then try to list all of the factors that could explain why a person might not be able to do these. When you have a list, look back over the health models in this chapter, labelling each of your reasons as a component of the models. How would you go about solving the barriers to action you have identified in each case? How many of them would involve needing more money or more time, and how many are related to personality?

EVALUATIVE COMMENT

Theories of lifestyle change emphasise the importance of attitudes in shaping behaviour. However, the link between behaviour and attitudes in the other direction has been less well explored. Does behaving in a certain way lead you to believe that it is a good thing, or at least not a bad thing? Bennett and Clatworthy (1999) demonstrate exactly how this may occur. Theirs was a study of women who smoked during pregnancy. They found that those who continued to smoke while carrying a child were less likely to agree with statements that stressed the harm that smoking can do to their baby. However, even these women had reduced the number of cigarettes that they smoked, which seems contradictory given that they deny the harmful effects it may have on their child.

The authors suggest that actual dependence on nicotine was an important modifying factor. These women were addicted to nicotine, and so felt that giving up completely was not a viable option for them. Their answer to this was to cut down smoking, rather than cut it out, but to deny the harm it may cause. This can be seen as a protective strategy. Although it does not protect physical health, it may protect mental health because the women concerned do not have to face the stress of knowing that they are smoking but are damaging their baby. By denying the harmful effects, they have let their behaviour shape their attitudes in a way that reduces any contradictions in their life.

EVALUATIVE COMMENT

In this chapter there are many examples of how health psychologists have attempted to understand health behaviours, and why some people do things that are detrimental to their health. It is clear that people are complicated, and that any attempt to pin down just one or two factors to explain behaviour is unlikely to succeed. As health psychology grows, more and more elaborate models are needed to enable health psychologists to predict behaviour, and to allow for the development of effective and efficient programmes of therapy to change behaviour and create a healthier world.

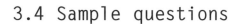

3.4 Sample questions

SAMPLE QUESTION

(a)   Outline one positive and one negative effect of exercise on health.

　　　(AO1 = 4)　　　　　　　　　　　　　　　　　　　　　　　　　　*(4 marks)*

(b)   Karen has tried to go on a diet numerous times in the past five years. When she goes on a diet she starts very strictly but tends to give up after the first few days. Explain one reason why Karen might find dieting difficult, and briefly suggest how she might diet more successfully.

　　　(AO1 = 2, AO2 = 2)　　　　　　　　　　　　　　　　　　　　*(4 marks)*

(c)   Discuss the role of diet in either cancer or cardiovascular disorder.

　　　(AO1 = 4, AO2 = 8)　　　　　　　　　　　　　　　　　　　　*(12 marks)*

　　　Total AO1 marks = 10　Total AO2 marks = 10　Total = 20 marks

QUESTIONS, ANSWERS AND COMMENTS

(a)   Explain how one behavioural risk factor is associated with one named ill-health condition.

　　　(AO1 = 1, AO2 = 2)　　　　　　　　　　　　　　　　　　　　*(3 marks)*

(b)   Outline and briefly discuss the use of media appeals in the primary prevention of illnesses associated with behavioural risk factors.

　　　(AO1 = 3, AO2 = 2)　　　　　　　　　　　　　　　　　　　　*(5 marks)*

(c)   Describe and discuss one theory of lifestyle change.

　　　(AO1 = 6, AO2 = 6)　　　　　　　　　　　　　　　　　　　　*(12 marks)*

　　　Total AO1 marks = 10　Total AO2 marks = 10　Total = 20 marks

Answer to (a)

One behavioural risk factor is smoking, which can cause cancer but does not always cause cancer in all smokers.

Comment: This answer gains just one mark as there is no explanation as to how smoking might cause cancer.

Answer to (b)

Media appeals have been used to inform people about the dangers of taking risks that might lead to illnesses like AIDS and cancer. Television can be used as a means of communicating about the dangers and can help target a specific audience by giving the information at certain times on certain channels. Studies have found that the sexual behaviour of gay communities, for example, can be changed significantly using media appeals, leading to a decrease in the spread of the virus. Care must be taken not to arouse too much fear in a media appeal as research shows that high fear arousal is less effective than moderate fear arousal in changing behaviour. In a review of results from the USA, Stall *et al.* (1988) said that AIDS campaigns had led to 'profound modifications' in health-related behaviour.

Comment: This answer was awarded four marks out of the five available. There is identification of an appropriate medium and a specific target audience for AO1, and discussion about the issue of fear arousal for two AO2 marks.

Answer to (c)

There are several theories of lifestyle change and here we shall consider the theory of planned behaviour, sometimes called the theory of reasoned action. Ajzen (1985) suggested that people are able to change their behaviour if they intend to change it and believe they are in control of what they do. For example, if someone intends to stop drinking alcohol and believes they are in control of their alcohol intake, then this gives them the ability to stop drinking or reduce the amount of alcohol they drink. The intentions and feeling of control work along with two other factors to determine whether or not people do change their behaviour.

First, norms or what is usual in society. For example, if someone wants to control alcohol intake they might consider their own intake in relation to what other people around them in society drink. If they see that others drink much less then there will be greater motivation and intention to change behaviour.

Second, attitudes work in conjunction with intention and perceived control. For example, if someone has a positive attitude towards drinking, thinking that it is something that sociable people do after work, then reduction of alcohol intake may be less likely even if the person intends to stop drinking and thinks they are in control of their drinking behaviour.

The theory of planned behaviour was supported by a study of Schifter and Ajzen (1985), who looked at weight loss and dieting in female students. They found that intention to lose weight alone did not necessarily lead to weight loss, but that those women who were most successful on the diets were those who believed they could eat less and could lose weight.

Other theories of lifestyle change are similar in important ways to the theory of planned behaviour and so support it to some extent. For example, a key feature of self-efficacy theory (Bandura) is the idea that people who want to change their lifestyle need to believe they can act, and act beneficially, if they are to be motivated to change. This type of belief is similar to the 'belief about control' element of planned behaviour theory.

One problem with the theory of planned behaviour is that what a person intends to do and what they actually do can be quite different. Another problem is that it takes no account of how people have behaved in the past – for example, whether people have tried in the past to stop drinking and failed. Being a cognitive-based theory it also neglects other factors in risk-taking such as the possibility that there may be a genetic predisposition to drinking alcohol. An inability to stop drinking alcohol might also be explained through behaviourist theory using the concepts of conditioning and positive reinforcement, and through social learning theory as in modelling.

Comment: This answer includes a thorough description of an appropriate theory with understanding of elements of the theory clearly evident in the example running through the whole of the answer. This application via use of example is awarded an AO2 mark. The description in the first three paragraphs is awarded four AO1 marks. Knowledge of evidence to support the theory is credited as AO1, and the comparison with Bandura's self-efficacy theory is awarded AO2 marks. Notice how this alternative theory is integrated into the answer as a whole and used in the context of evaluation rather than presented as an 'add-on', as often happens when candidates give alternatives to a theory or model under discussion. There are several valid points made rather briefly in the final paragraph. Had these been expanded the answer would have gained more marks but because of its brevity, the total number of AO2 marks awarded for this question is five. Thus the answer gains a total of 10 marks out of the 12 available.

3.5 FURTHER READING

Introductory texts

Forshaw, M. 2002b: **Essential Health Psychology**. Arnold, London

Taylor, S.E. 2003: **Health Psychology** 5th Ed. McGraw-Hill, Boston

Specialist sources

Conner, M. and Norman, P. (eds) 1995: **Predicting Health Behaviour.** Open University Press, Buckingham

Rutter, D. and Quine, L. (eds) 2002: **Changing Health Behaviour.** Open University Press, Buckingham

4

Stress and stress management

4.1 Stress and illness

The nature of stress

Stress is, arguably, the most researched and documented area of health psychology and the main area of interest for many health psychologists. Take any medical condition and stress will probably have been shown to make it worse. Efforts to combat stress represent a massive industry around the world, of which health psychology is a tiny part. Probably the biggest sector of this industry is the sale of 'stress-busting' books, relaxation tapes, exercise videos, and the like. Stress affects almost everyone at some time, and is a permanent underlying factor in the lives of many people. Have you ever known anyone who would say that they have never experienced stress? Stress is also unusual in that it can cause itself. If you are aware of your stress symptoms then this awareness is quite likely to increase your stress. Thus, a cycle is established that is difficult to break.

Stress is normal, in that all human beings experience it at some time

Mechanic (1978) pointed out that stress can lead to increased use of health-care resources, not only because stress genuinely causes ill-health, but also because stressed people are more worried and concerned about their health, even when they need not be. A slight pain can seem more serious to a stressed person. Mood is known to have a significant effect on the reporting of symptoms. Someone who is in a negative mood is more likely to report pain, for instance, than a happier person. Salovey and Birnbaum (1989) studied people with influenza or influenza symptoms and used a short procedure to alter their mood experimentally. The people put into a negative mood reported twice as many aches and pains as those in the positive or neutral mood conditions.

Stress leads to increased heart rate and hypertension. Hypertension is thought to be a factor in deaths from cardiovascular disease. Thus, stress is a serious issue for study. Here we concentrate on the psychological research into its direct effects on the lives of people, and how stress can be relieved.

Measuring stress

SELF-REPORT TECHNIQUES

A great deal of effort has been put into measuring and cataloguing stress and there are many stress scales in existence. One of the earliest and most famous attempts to measure and catalogue stress came from Holmes and Rahe (1967). They gave a large number of participants a list of events that occur in everyday life, and asked the participants to rate them as to how difficult they would be for a person to adjust to. The implication was that the more stressful something was, the more difficult it would be to adjust to it. The list of potential **stressors** included death of a partner, moving house, going to jail, experiencing Christmas and becoming pregnant. By averaging over the responses, a points system was developed, such that each stressor in a person's life was attached to a certain number of points. By adding up the points, one could see how much stress a person was experiencing.

EVALUATIVE COMMENT

This rather crude approach was soon criticised. First, no attempt was made to account for the differences between individuals. Death of a partner was listed as the most stressful of events, gaining a score of 100 points. However, age and partner's age, and the nature of the relationship, and the reason for death, can all interact to affect the level of stress perceived by the individual. In addition, the additive nature of the scale meant that experiencing a set of difficulties often added up to equivalent stress as that felt when experiencing one major stressor. For example, moving to a smaller house (25 points) and changing one's eating habits (15 points) is as stressful, therefore, as becoming pregnant (40 points).

Naturally, the points system would make little sense to the real people to whom these things are happening. Finally, a significant drawback of the social readjustment rating scale (SRRS) is that it fails to make allowance for the world of difference between a positive and a negative stressor. Going on holiday is stressful, true, but it is also something people want. The same usually applies to moving house. Then there are those stressors that can be positive or negative depending upon the circumstances: some people are glad to be pregnant, others are not; some people are devastated by divorce, others celebrate. However, the SRRS set the agenda for health psychologists to develop more sophisticated tools for the description and measurement of stress.

Life is made up of 'big things' and 'little things' that happen to us. Ask yourself how many big things happen to you in a year, and then think about how many little things happen. No matter how you choose to define 'big' and 'little', you will probably have to admit that very few big things happen, but that it is perhaps impossible to count all of the little things. A great deal of our stress comes from the little things that happen. Think about how often you find yourself thinking or saying something like 'that bugs me', 'it really winds me up', 'how annoying!' or 'that gets on my nerves'.

PRACTICAL Activity

Try this on your own or in a group. Write down as many of life's 'minor hassles' as you can think of. If you are working with others, you can compare lists and discuss whether you agree on each of them. Try to give each one a mark from 1 to 100 as to how stressful you perceive it to be. Reflect on how difficult it is to decide on a mark for each.

Kanner *et al.* (1981) developed the **hassles scale** to try to measure stress caused by little things. Stress from these minor stressors could add up to a significant health problem. They might include having to queue at the bank, feeling fat, waiting for a friend to call, wishing that you could give up smoking, arguing with a family member, or any number of other possibilities. Of course, life isn't just made up of negative things; good things happen too. Because life is a mixture of good things and bad things, sometimes the bad things do not feel as bad as they might because a good thing happened. Kanner *et al.* therefore included a second scale in their study, measuring what they called 'uplifts'. By taking into account scores from both hassles and uplifts, it was hoped that a better overall assessment of experienced stress could be gained. People were given the hassles and uplifts scale along with measures of psychological factors such as depression and anxiety. Over a period of nine months, the authors found that hassles were much better predictors of psychological health than were major events.

EVALUATIVE COMMENT

One of the problems with the measurement of daily hassles as an index of stress is of a 'chicken or egg' nature. Daily hassles might in themselves be stressful, but equally they might be perceived as stressful only because the person is already stressed by something else (which could be some major life event, as measured by Holmes and Rahe). Therefore, major life events may be the main determinants of stress, and daily hassles might simply follow from that. That is, daily hassles are not particularly stressful in themselves, but they may take on much greater impact when the person is already stressed. Kanner *et al.* (1981) performed a statistical technique to assess the relationship between major life events and daily hassles and stress, and discovered that even after major life events had been taken out of the equation, minor

Much of the stress we experience comes from the little irritations in life, like having to wait when we are in a hurry

events like hassles still predicted psychological health. Therefore, a combination of major and minor stressors, 'softened' by pleasurable and relaxing experiences, seems to determine our stress status.

So far, we have talked about self-report measures of stress. In many ways these are the most important measures we have. We can argue that it does not matter if a person is genuinely in a stressful situation. If a person *feels* stressed, then they *are* stressed. Sometimes we might, however, be interested in other measures of stress, perhaps to compare them with self-reported stress. This is when we might look at physiological or behavioural measures.

PHYSIOLOGICAL MEASURES

The body responds to stress in a variety of ways that are detailed later in this chapter. Although all of these bodily changes could be used as measures of stress, not all are easily measurable. There are, however, some physiological changes that can be measured reasonably easily. Blood or urine samples can be analysed for levels of hormones present in the body, and these levels can be monitored to determine both immediate reactions to stress-inducing events and long-term stress. Two types of hormones – corticosteroids and catecholamines, including epinephrine and norepinephrine – are secreted by the adrenal glands. Mechanical means of detecting stress-induced changes include blood-pressure and heart-rate monitors and galvanic skin response (GSR) meters that detect changes in the surface moisture of the skin associated with an alarm reaction. These measures are often combined in a polygraph apparatus to simultaneously record changes in heart rate, blood pressure and GSR.

EVALUATIVE COMMENT

Although physiological measures are highly objective and can be recorded accurately they are not always as useful as they might first appear. The major problem is that the body becomes aroused for a variety of reasons, so, although increased heart rate, blood pressure and GSR can accurately and reliably be detected, it is not possible to determine from the physiological changes alone exactly what emotion is being experienced. In many cases the broad physiological reaction to an anxiety-provoking event, such as an argument at work, may be very similar to the bodily reaction to a pleasantly arousing event, such as receiving a much-desired birthday gift. Sarafino (1994) suggests other disadvantages of physiological measures: they require technical equipment and thus are expensive; the procedure itself may actually induce stress in the person being measured; they are affected by variables such as gender, body weight, prior activity and previously ingested substances such as caffeine.

BEHAVIOURAL MEASURES

Behavioural measures of stress involve observation of a person's behaviour to see whether they are acting in a manner consistent with that of a person experiencing stress. Stressed people often talk more quickly and less coherently, they become less patient. Sometimes they become more aggressive, and occasionally, under extreme or long-term stress will experience a 'breakdown', where they will act in an unusual manner, seemingly helpless and confused. By measuring behaviour like this we supposedly achieve an objective measure of stress. Taking a behavioural measure of stress such as speech rate or the number of speech errors is more meaningful if there is information about the person's normal rate of speech and how many speech errors they make in normal conversation. Thus, an experimental study involving the use of a control condition would be necessary when taking a behavioural measure of stress.

PRACTICAL Activity

Make a list of the ways in which stress might show itself in a person's behaviour. You can start with rate of speech and number of speech errors. What other sorts of non-verbal clues to stress might be apparent from how someone behaves? When you think your list is complete watch a TV news programme that includes a tricky interview with a politician. See how many observable signs of stress occur and whether you need to add to or delete from your list.

Biological systems and stress

Stress is not just something that happens to the mind. In fact, it is just as much about the body. We will now look at two physical systems that are relevant to our understanding of stress.

THE ENDOCRINE SYSTEM

Glands that produce hormones are called endocrine glands. Much of our behaviour occurs in some part because of hormones circulating in our bodies that have particular effects, not only on tissues all over the body but specifically in the brain itself. Hormones are chemicals that regulate processes within the body. They are responsible for hunger, thirst, sexual appetite, and so on. If you alter the body's hormonal content, you create, in many respects, a different *person*. To an extent, health psychologists focus on personalities and the cognitions and emotions associated with those personalities.

The **endocrine system** includes the following structures: the hypothalamus, the pineal and pituitary glands, the thyroid, the liver, kidney, pancreas and adrenal gland, the ovaries and the testes. Without hormones, many necessary, normal functions and activities, such as growth during the life span and sexual maturation, would not occur. When hormonal levels are changed, illness and unusual behaviour can result. Hormonal levels may change because of *endogenous* or *exogenous* factors.

Endogenous factors are events or processes originating *within* the body. For instance, a tumour in the pituitary gland might affect the production of TSH (thyroid-stimulating hormone). This would then affect the amount of thyroxine produced by the thyroid gland in the neck. As a result, a person might suffer from an underactive or overactive thyroid (known as *hypothyroidism* and *hyperthyroidism* respectively). Both of these affect behaviour. In the case of hypothyroidism (also called myxoedema) a lack of thyroxine can lead to sluggishness, weight gain, deepening of the voice and slowness of speech. Hyperthyroidism (thyrotoxicosis) is caused by too much thyroxine circulating in the body. Among other things, the person loses weight, their heart beats faster, and they appear agitated and anxious. They can even become noticeably more aggressive. In both cases, the changes in behaviour are enough for people to notice that the person is not 'being themselves'; they are behaving differently. Not only this, but they are experiencing more stress as a result, and their loved ones may experience that stress too.

Exogenous factors originate *outside* of the body. Certain toxins, for example, would be considered exogenous causes. Chronic (long-term) alcohol poisoning can lead to cirrhosis (degeneration) of the liver, which in turn can cause atrophy (shrinkage) of the testes. A consequence of this is infertility. Since the testicles produce the androgen testosterone (a hormone), which is responsible for 'masculine' sexual characteristics, diminishing production of testosterone can create erectile dysfunction and a loss of libido. Think about how stressful it can be for people when they want children and cannot have them, or want sex but are unable to 'perform'. Thus, the body can cause stress when it fails to act normally.

THE NERVOUS SYSTEM

This highly complex system contains the brain, which alone is made up of billions of cells with billions of connections (synapses). The nervous system is responsible for the co-ordination of all of the other systems, making it the body's control centre. The nervous system divides into two sub-systems: the **central nervous system** (CNS) and the **peripheral nervous system** (PNS). The PNS is itself divided into two further sub-systems: the somatic nervous system and the autonomic nervous system. Confusingly, the autonomic nervous system is further divided into the sympathetic and parasympathetic systems!

The CNS consists of the brain and the spinal cord. The spinal cord is the structure that enables communication with the body parts below the head. Clinical psychologists in particular spend a lot of their time working with patients who have, either because of trauma or surgery, suffered damage to the CNS. Strokes and physical accidents are common causes of change of mood and behaviour, and often affect everyday abilities such as speech.

The PNS is made up of nerve cells and nerve bundles outside of the CNS. As stated earlier, it divides into the somatic nervous system and the autonomic nervous system. The somatic nervous system is the mode of transport for 'messages' from the CNS to the muscles and glands, and from the sense organs to the CNS. When you touch something, the signals relating to that experience reach the brain via the somatic nervous system. Select a body part – your eyes, arm,

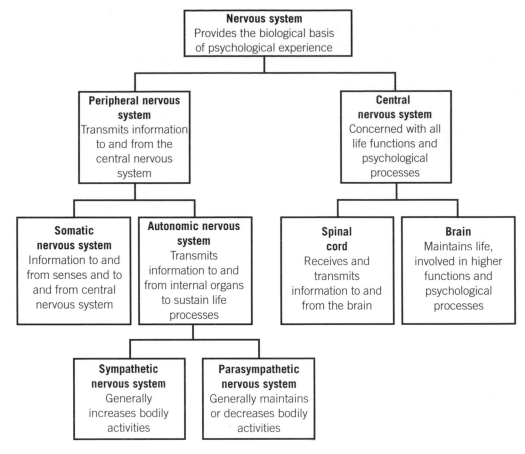

Figure 4.1: Structure and functions of the nervous system (reproduced, with permission, from Pennington, 2002)

fingers, whatever – and move it, any way that you choose. The brain enables you to do this, and uses the somatic nervous system to send the right messages to your muscles to make it happen. The autonomic nervous system includes the nerve cells responsible for controlling the beating of the heart and the action of the intestines. To summarise: the heart is part of the cardiovascular system and the intestines are part of the digestive/excretory system; both are activated by the autonomic nervous system, which is part of the peripheral nervous system.

So we now need to turn to the two divisions of the autonomic nervous system: the sympathetic nervous system and the parasympathetic nervous system. In our world, we need a train to take us to work, and we need another to take us home again. The sympathetic and parasympathetic systems act together like this. The sympathetic system prepares us to face danger, either by standing up to it or by running away (the **fight-or-flight response**). It makes our heart beat more quickly and makes us breathe more heavily. It may slow down the activity of the digestive system (when you are running for your life away from a predator it does not make sense for your body to be using up valuable energy digesting your recent sandwich). Conversely, the parasympathetic nervous system slows down the heart rate and increases digestive activity (once you have got safely away from the predator, you need to calm down, rest and allow your body to regain strength by turning the sandwich into energy). However, it is important to realise that this does not mean that the two systems work in alternation – one on/one off – and then vice versa. In fact, both are working to some extent all of the time. The temporary, relative power of one over the other is what makes things happen a particular way. In a sense, the systems constantly work together, but are also constantly in opposition. Sometimes, however, they simply co-operate to produce one ultimate effect. For example, in males, the parasympathetic system is responsible for erection of the penis, whereas the sympathetic system co-ordinates ejaculation.

The sympathetic nervous system, as already mentioned, is responsible for the fight-or-flight response that is the basis for the stress response. Cannon (1927) described the reactions of the body to danger, suggesting why these have evolved. The blood pressure and heart rate increase, and the person sweats. The digestive system partly shuts down. Today, few people are likely to be chased by a tiger while engaging in their daily activities. Nowadays dangers are more subtle: divorce, redundancy, unemployment, petty crime, debt, sexual dysfunction, nuisance neighbours, legal disputes. These are the things that people fear today, and these are the things that cause anxiety and stress. The bodily signs of stress include increased blood pressure, increased heart rate, digestive problems, and so on. This is the irony of the stress response; it is a necessary, acute reaction to a potentially harmful situation, but chronically it can be fatal.

THE STRESS RESPONSE

Health psychologists have a particular interest in responses to stress. Disorders in biological systems can generate stress, and stress can create disorders in systems.

Stress is the natural response to a danger or concern that an organism faces, and prepares the organism for potential trouble. Stress is what happens to a person when they are in 'fight-or-flight' response mode. When danger is faced, or anticipated, the following effects occur.

- Heart rate changes, and strength of heartbeat changes. Usually, both increase, but the opposite may happen. In the most common situation, the heart rate changes to allow more blood to be pumped around the body quickly. What the person perceives is a fast pulse and, often, very rapid heart beat or palpitations. Palpitations are a sign of stress.

- Blood pressure increases. While it is usual for people not to notice blood pressure changes directly (although some people do say that they can feel this, especially after a heavy meal), they tend to notice the consequences of blood pressure increases such as headaches. It is hardly surprising, then, that headaches are a classic symptom of stress.

- Blood vessels in skin alter in girth. At highly stressful times they narrow or constrict. Constriction serves the purpose of directing blood towards the muscles and organs that require it as a priority. As a result, people may go much paler than they usually are. In lesser emergencies, the blood vessels will open up or dilate, and the person becomes flushed and more pink. Black people undergo exactly the same changes, but they are generally less noticeable than in white people.

- Muscles become prepared for action by increased blood flow to them. Stressed people are said to be 'tense', and may require methods such as massage to loosen up the muscles the body has put into a state of preparation for activity, in anticipation of trouble.

- Sweat glands begin to work harder. This cools the body down to prevent overheating. However, the stressed person (and their friends and family) may notice that they have more body odour than previously. The person may notice that deodorants don't seem to work as well for them as they used to. They may be noticeably wet on the brow, or under the arms or on the back.

- Lungs can take in more air because the air passages open up. Stressed people may breathe unevenly, perhaps taking in deeper breaths than might seem necessary. The frequency of sighing might be increased. As a result of increased activity, the lungs might become sensitive, causing them to shut off; asthma is something that is more likely to be found in people who are anxious and stressed.

- The pupils of the eyes dilate. This allows more light to be let in, thus giving the eyes a better chance of picking out danger. However, to other people, this may look strange. The stare of a stressed person can be quite different from that of a relaxed one.

- Salivation is temporarily turned off. Generally, the body does not need saliva during a dangerous situation. The body's energy is better used on other things. Therefore, the mouth becomes dry. Dryness of the mouth is another sign of stress.

- Digestive processes are altered. Depending on the nature of the situation, food in the stomach may need to be held there until later, or it may need to be digested quickly. In the former case, it is kept in the stomach longer than usual, and in the latter increased secretions of gastric acids can lead to damage to the stomach itself. That is why it is not unusual for people with chronic stress problems to develop stomach ulcers.

- Intestinal activity is changed. Again, the situation may call for a suspension of bowel activity or it might call for increased attention to it. If the dangerous situation is pre-empted, it makes sense for the body to get rid of waste. Running away from a predator is easier if you are a few ounces lighter. Thus diarrhoea can occur. However, if the danger is immediate, the system is designed to stop bowel activity, thus saving energy for fight or flight. As a consequence, constipation occurs. Irregularity in the function of the bowels is another classic symptom of stress.

Given what happens to a stressed body, it is easy to see how long-term bouts of stress can place considerable strain upon the biological systems and often damage them irreparably. Stress is a major source of health problems in many countries.

Interestingly, small amounts of stress might be good for a person, since they can be viewed as a form of 'exercise' of the cardiovascular and respiratory systems. Moderate exercise is beneficial precisely because it makes us breathe more quickly and more deeply, and it causes the blood pressure to temporarily rise, the heart rate to increase, and so on. Therefore, occasional stress can be a form of moderate exercise. Positive stress is often termed **eustress**.

A little stress now and then can be good for us

PRACTICAL Activity

Write down as many examples of eustress as you can. When you have the list, think of which of them are social activities and which solitary ones. Would these change from stress to eustress, or vice versa, when you add or take away other people? For example, watching a horror movie might be eustress when at the cinema. Watching a horror movie at home alone might be stress.

EVALUATIVE COMMENT

Psychoneuroimmunology is a relatively new field of psychological medicine. It has caught the imagination of many health psychologists because it involves a strong and explicit recognition of the relationship between mind and body. The immune system itself is vital in the upkeep of the human body. It is responsible for defending the body against bacteria and viruses, and is also implicated in diseases such as cancer. There is now evidence that the functioning of the immune system (immunocompetence) can be affected by the workings of the mind, with a link between stress and the immune response. Studies suggest that the immune system works less well when a person is undergoing stress. Anything that adversely affects the immune system certainly weakens the organism.

Study 4.1

AIM Cohen, Tyrrell and Smith (1993) set out to study the effects of infection by the common cold virus, comparing people who reported having had a number of significantly stressful life events with those who had not.

METHOD An experimental group was deliberately infected with the common cold virus while members of a placebo group were told that they might have been infected by the virus although they had not been exposed to it at all. Following actual or supposed exposure to the virus, participants were assessed on a number of measures, including body temperature and amount of nasal mucus.

RESULTS After infection with the virus under controlled conditions those people who had reported more stressful events in the previous year had higher temperatures than those who had experienced less stress. They also reported more nasal mucus, one of the characteristic signs of having a cold, as the reader will be aware. These were not purely psychogenic symptoms. The members of the placebo group that was not subjected to the cold virus (but who *thought* that they *might* have been) did not develop these symptoms, even if they were people who had reported high levels of stress in the 12 months prior to the study.

CONCLUSION Common-sense notions that when bad things happen to people it toughens them up were not supported. If anything, stress appears to have the opposite effect, such that if a person becomes ill, stressful events can make their illness worse.

Stress can affect the functioning of the immune system in two ways: physiologically, through chemical effects; behaviourally, through people's responses to stress, which can then damage the body further. Not only does stress cause chemicals to be released that can affect immunocompetence, but also a person who is stressed is more likely to smoke, drink alcohol, take other drugs and eat poorly, all of which have an impact on immunocompetence.

The role of personal variables in stress

BEHAVIOUR TYPE

Friedman and Rosenman (1974) suggested that people with a certain personality type tended to be more predisposed to suffer from stress than other types. The Type A person was identified as exhibiting the following characteristics: competitive achievement orientation leading to extreme self-criticism; time urgency leading to a constant struggle against the clock and a compulsion to try to do more than one thing at a time; anger/hostility that may or may not be openly expressed. Friedman and Rosenman (1974) compared the personality characteristics and behavioural styles of patients suffering from heart disease with those exhibited in non-patients. They found that heart disease patients were much more likely than non-patients to show Type A characteristics and behaviours. A contrasting type was also identified – a **Type B personality** – who tended to show the opposite characteristics to Type A people, being more easy-going and much less demanding of self and others.

Study 4.2

AIM Friedman and Rosenman (1959) attempted to establish a link between behaviour patterns and coronary heart disease. Previous research had suggested that a prime cause of coronary heart disease was an excessive need to compete, and stress at work.

METHOD Three groups of men were compared. Group A comprised 83 men, identified by their work colleagues as competitive, desiring success, intensely driven, aware of deadline pressure, always in a rush, and extremely mentally and physically alert. Group B comprised 83 men matched for age and physical characteristics but showing the opposite behaviours to Group A. Group C comprised 46 visually impaired men with low drive and ambition, and severe insecurity. Each group was interviewed about several issues, including family history, illnesses, work, sleep, exercise, diet and alcohol consumption. Several measures of cardiovascular function were taken, including cholesterol levels and electrocardiogram readings.

RESULTS Group A men were found to work longer hours and be more active than Group B men, and to be more likely to have a family history of heart disease. On all risk factors, Group A men were judged to be five times more likely than Group B men to be at risk of developing heart disease.

CONCLUSION Men displaying Type A behaviour patterns are more likely to be at risk of developing coronary heart disease. Friedman and Rosenman further concluded that Type A behaviours may be partly inherited. Thus, Type A should be viewed not only as a pattern of behaviours occurring in certain people as a response to stress, but also as a source of stress from within a person with that type of personality.

Since Friedman and Rosenman (1959) first identified the Type A personality there has been extensive research into the relationship between Type A behaviour, stress and stress-related illnesses. Type A individuals have been found to show a greater physiological response to stress or 'reactivity', demonstrated in increased blood pressure, heart rate and plasma catecholamine levels. Interestingly, it has been found that Type A behaviours may in part be due to the physiological reactivity that Type A people show. Krantz et al. (1982) showed how Type A people taking beta-blockers, a type of drug that acts to subdue the activity of the nervous system, showed less Type A behaviour in assessments than a control group of Type A people not prescribed beta-blockers.

EVALUATIVE COMMENT

Type A personality can be assessed in a number of ways but most usually involves the use of a structured interview, where a trained interviewer asks questions about behaviour patterns and characteristics such as competitiveness and hostility. The interview involves deliberate attempts to annoy the interviewee, for example, with undue prolonged pauses on the part of the researcher, to see how the interviewee responds to such provocation. Responses to frustration, such as sighing, are recorded. The recordings are then analysed and rated by an independent researcher, who determines classification as either Type A or B. The structured interview approach includes measures of all aspects of Type A and results usually correlate well with health status in relation to heart disease. One limitation of the structured interview is the amount of time taken to carry out the interview in relation to self-report methods.

LOCUS OF CONTROL

The links between personal control, perceived or actual, and health have been studied by health psychologists interested in stress. According to Rotter (1966), **locus of control** is the extent to which a person feels that they are able to make a difference to things around them and to their own life circumstances. Helplessness might, therefore, be argued to be the extreme opposite of control. When attempting to explain events in our lives and our own behaviour there are two possible types of explanation: those with an internal locus of control make internal attributions, explaining what happens to them as due to their own actions; those with an external locus of control make external attributions, explaining what happens to them as being outside their control.

Whether or not we have a tendency to make internal or external attributions can have a profound effect on the amount of stress experienced and the type of life choices we make. For example, a woman who tends to make external attributions might believe that there is no point going to college to take any qualifications because she will never be able to get a good job. As a result she will feel stressed, unhappy and helpless. On the other hand, a woman who makes internal attributions might enrol on a course to get qualifications that will enable her to get a better job. Even if things don't work out exactly as planned, she will feel more positive, believing that she can have some influence over what happens in her life.

PRACTICAL Activity

Make a list of statements about the following situations. For each situation, think of a statement that might be made by a person with an internal locus of control and one that might be made by a person with an external locus of control.

- Being 'dumped' by a boyfriend or girlfriend.

- Going for an interview and not getting the job.

- Living next door to a very noisy neighbour.

Now think about how the different attributions made by people with either an internal or an external locus of control might affect the amount of stress they experience in these situations.

One of the most common areas of study for the link between health, stress and control is the realm of work. People are often stressed by work, and they are equally often lacking control over the nature of the work. After all, it is rare that someone can do more or less what they like at work. Someone else usually controls the work done and the way that it is done. The very phrase 'quality control' gives away the sense in which work is usually directed by other people. Someone produces, someone else controls for the quality of what is produced, often by creating more and more rules for people to work by.

Study 4.3

AIM Frankenhaeuser (1975) examined control and stress in a sample of sawmill workers in Sweden. The work was monotonous and unvaried with the same action repeated over and over again, day after day, for often a whole working life.

METHOD Frankenhaeuser measured the biochemical effects of stress, taking levels of catecholamines in the blood. Blood-pressure levels and self-report measures of headaches and digestive problems were also recorded.

RESULTS Frankenhaeuser found that the sawmill workers had significantly higher than normal levels of catecholamines, which are associated with stress. They also showed more than average signs of stress for hypertension, headaches and digestive tract problems.

CONCLUSION These workers were experiencing high levels of stress because of the nature of their work. The key fact here is that the workers have no say in anything they do, and so feel like their work is entirely out of their control.

EVALUATIVE COMMENT

For most people, lack of control over certain aspects of life can be a demoralising process that affects stress levels and, hence, health. Of course, we must not forget that there are probably people for whom control itself is stressful. Not everyone wants responsibility. In fact, the evidence shows that too much control can also be a bad thing. Other typically high-stress occupations include management, medicine, law and teaching. Here people often have high degrees of autonomy. The stress in these occupations is often attributed to the pressure created by being responsible and in charge. Being the person who can be blamed when things go wrong can be just as stressful as never having a say in what happens.

HARDINESS

Hardiness is a concept first put forward by Kobasa (1979), which describes a set of traits that can protect a person from the effects of stress, and that includes control as a factor. This is a personality-based approach, which focuses on characteristics of the individual rather than of the environment. Contrast this with the previous information on social support. A 'hardy' person copes well with stress. According to Kobasa, hardy people have a high sense of personal control (believing that they can *do* things about their life and health), and are committed to things. They like challenges, seeing challenge as a good thing in life. The hardy person views change as a positive rather than a negative thing, employing what is described as a **positive reappraisal** coping strategy. With respect to commitment, the hardy person values and finds purpose in their work and their social contacts. A hardy person is often a resilient individual, the type of person about which people say 'she can cope with anything'. They are the survivors of this world, the people who seem to 'take whatever is thrown at them'; they are the people who 'bounce back'.

Hardiness is generally measured using a combination of scales measuring each of the individual components of reaction to change, control and commitment. There is a moderate amount of evidence to show that hardiness acts as a buffer against stress, although the evidence is countered by studies showing little effect of hardiness, as defined by Kobasa, on reactions to stress.

One problem with hardiness is that the factors that comprise it are not always found together in the same person. They do not correlate very highly with each other, which they should if hardiness can be seen as *one* collective thing. Of course, the counter-argument could be that hardy individuals are those people in whom high levels of these three factors *are* found.

EVALUATIVE COMMENT

It is sometimes suggested that women are generally more hardy than men and cope better with stress. Health psychologists have been guilty, over the years, of concentrating on a male-oriented view of stress and its effects (Carroll and Niven, 1993). There is evidence that men and women differ in their reactions to stress, and in their general levels of perceived stress. Of course, most societies treat men and women differently, and so we cannot know whether these differences are due to the social and cultural variation between the sexes or to biological differences. In an important early paper, Waldron (1976) argues that women live longer than men because men often cope with stress in ways that are harmful, such as smoking cigarettes and excess drinking of alcohol. You may, however, be aware that, in the UK at least, the incidence of smoking in females is increasing, while in men it is not, and that a similar pattern of drinking behaviour to that seen in men is starting to become apparent in young women.

Whether the gender-biased coping strategy identified by Waldron will remain in even just a few years seems doubtful.

Interpersonal factors as mediators of stress

A key factor in reducing stress, or at least in cutting down on the effects that stress can have on the person, is social support. Social support is the term given by psychologists not only to support given through friendships and family, but also to that from professionals and any significant others. Generally it can come in five forms, although some researchers suggest overlap between them. The main categories are **appraisal support**, **emotional support**, **esteem support**, **informational support** and **instrumental support** (Stroebe, 2000).

- Appraisal support is where a person is enabled or encouraged to understand and evaluate their own state of health or problem-state, perhaps through provision of information and empowerment. They are then able to put their stressors into context.

- Emotional support is being loved, cared for, protected, listened to, empathised and sympathised with. It is what people often mean when they say that they have a 'shoulder to cry on'.

- Esteem support is a feeling that you are valued, or held in esteem, by others. Your own feelings of self-worth and self-esteem are affected by how you perceive others' opinions of you. If you feel that you are a competent and skilful person, a worthwhile person, a good person, you are more likely to be able to cope with demands put upon you, by stressors, for instance.

- Informational support is often provided in the first instance by a medical professional, in the case of health or illness. It is support in the form of advice and knowledge that can assist the person in doing the right thing to look after themselves. It also takes the form of feedback, so that attending special weight-loss classes, say, where you are weighed and told the result of your efforts is, among other things, a form of informational support.

- Instrumental support is much more down to earth and practical. You cannot attend a weight-loss class if you have no one to look after your children while you go, or if you have no money. If someone offers to pay for your visit, and will act as a baby-sitter too, then they have provided instrumental support.

Study 4.4

AIM Sosa *et al.* (1980) carried out a field experiment to study the effects of instrumental support on experiences of childbirth.

METHOD Expectant mothers were assigned at random to either an experimental or a control group. The women in the experimental group were accompanied throughout labour by an untrained helper/adviser who provided social support in the form of conversation and general care, but not nursing care – this was provided by hospital staff. The control group received nursing care only.

RESULTS Average labour time was much shorter for the experimental group (8.8 hours) than for the control group (19.3 hours).

CONCLUSION The instrumental social support relieved stress in the experimental-group mothers, making them less anxious and allowing for shorter labour.

A classic study into the effects of social support was reported by Berkman and Syme (1979). Thousands of people were followed over nine years in Alameda County, California. Data on social support was obtained from questions on marital status, attendance at church, contact with friends and family, and membership of organisations likely to bring the person into contact with others. In addition, self-reports of various health variables and behaviours were examined, such as tobacco and alcohol intake and exercise. The researchers discovered a direct relationship between amount of social support and death. Those people who received the most social support were least likely to die during the nine years, and those with least support were most likely to die. This interacted with age, such that older people with little social support were in a much more dangerous position than younger ones. This was a clear indicator that social support is directly related to health status.

The type of support available depends on the social network of the individual, their gender, their culture, and many other factors. Ideally an individual would have all types of support available whenever they are needed, but this is probably little more than an ideal. Most people will experience problems with social support at some point, even if only because of limited resources such as money. In different cultures, friendship and family networks operate in different ways. Extended-family cultures, such as those found in India, are more likely to generate instrumental support (because more people can provide more money and equipment), and esteem and emotional support can be provided by a range of people, thus meaning that none of them feel too much strain. Of course, we often say that 'too many cooks spoil the broth', and it is also possible that a large amount of support can be overwhelming or counterproductive for some individuals. Many of us will have known people getting married who started to resent the 'help' of their families because they feel like control is being taken away from them and that people are 'interfering'. Different situations will lead to different interpretations of the support offered by the social network. Indeed, when others offer help but it is not perceived as supportive then the effects of that support are unlikely to benefit the health of the individual and their perceived levels of stress (Dakof and Taylor, 1990).

Living here, in such poverty, can be a very unhealthy experience, but being surrounded by friendly supportive neighbours can help to counteract this

DIRECT AND BUFFERING HYPOTHESES

The effects of social support on health are seen via the stress-health link, where social support prevents stress from affecting health in the way that it otherwise might. There are two ways in which this can happen: directly or indirectly.

The **direct hypothesis**, sometimes referred to as the main effect model, is underpinned by a philosophy that social support is always a good thing, regardless of any stressors you are experiencing or the powerfulness of them. The more social support you have, the better. Social support affects your mental health, this in turn affects your physical health, and therefore you are shielded directly against oncoming stressors. In effect, the absence of social support is a stressor in itself.

According to the **buffering hypothesis**, the link between social support and relief from stress is indirect. Here the powerfulness of a stressor is important in determining the mediating effects of the social support. The 'buffer' of social support protects the individual against powerful stressors, but does not have much effect when the stressors are weaker. Rather than protect the person at all times, the social support they have really only works when they need it the most. This may seem rather vague, so let us take an example.

In everyday life, the things that stress us are the minor hassles like queuing in the rain for a taxi, replacement of our favourite TV programme with an extended news bulletin or leaving a set of lesson notes on the bus. The argument is that social support is unlikely to be of much use in these circumstances. We might mention to a friend that we got wet in the taxi queue, but we are unlikely to need or ask for 'tea and sympathy' and financial or informational support! However, imagine now that a couple lose a baby due to miscarriage. Friends and family may pay them more attention, help them with getting advice from doctors, counsellors and social workers (if appropriate), or do shopping for them if they feel too upset to undertake routine activities. A family member might pay for them to have a break abroad. The couple may feel that they are in some way responsible for the loss of their baby, and those around them could provide esteem support by countering these ideas when they are expressed. As can be seen, in drastic conditions this support could make a great difference.

EVALUATIVE COMMENT

Using twin study evidence, Kessler *et al.* (1992) suggest that people differ, genetically, in the way that they find and evaluate social support. Some people may be better at finding social support, and, when support is there, they are good at perceiving the assistance as supportive. The buffering effects of social support may, therefore, be due to a person being able to make use of social support when they need it – that is, in times of great stress. At other times, they don't need it, so it is not going to show up as a buffer. Equally, certain people may be good at creating a social support network when they need it. If they don't need it, during minor hassles, they don't set it up, and so it can hardly act as a buffer! Of course, not all people have the gift of drawing upon individuals and organisations effectively and efficiently when required. These are, perhaps, the people who most need skills training to reduce their stress.

4.2 Coping and stress management

Coping with stress is no different from coping with anything else, in that the ability to do so depends upon both physical and mental resources, and the culture and personality of the individual. Coping is an interesting phenomenon, since it can be a form of cure. In physical injury, such as a broken leg, successful coping will have, possibly, a small impact on the healing of the bone (via the immune system), but nothing more. However, coping with stressors is quite different. By coping with a stressor, a person removes its label as a stressor. Of course, if something isn't a

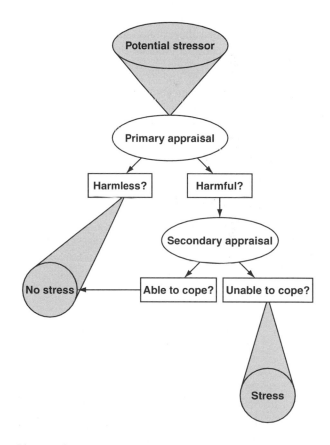

Figure 4.2: According to Lazarus (1966), two stages of appraisal determine stress

stressor, it can't cause stress. A lot depends upon how we appraise a situation. Lazarus (1966) developed a transactional model of stress, which featured appraisal of the stress as a process that occurs in two stages (see Figure 4.2).

Primary appraisal is the perception of an event as being either mainly harmful or harmless. Secondary appraisal is the individual's perception of their self-efficacy in dealing with the potential stressor. Events are therefore 'filtered'. Only an event that is perceived as potentially harmful, and where the person also believes that they are ill equipped to deal with it, will become a threat to the individual and likely to cause full-blown stress. Thus, by dealing with a stressful situation, or coping, it is possible to 'cure' the problem. In the case of non-physical difficulties, coping *is* the cure. For someone who is grieving over the death of a loved one, doctors cannot give 'grief drugs'. All that is really available is coping, which can be helped by other people, as we shall see.

Problem-focused and emotion-focused strategies

Coping strategies are often labelled as either problem-focused or emotion-focused. **Problem-focused coping** involves dealing with the problem itself, whereas **emotion-focused coping** is centred on the emotional reaction to the problem.

Study 4.5

AIM Billings and Moos (1981) assessed whether people tended to prefer problem- or emotion-focused strategies.

METHOD A total of 200 married couples completed a survey about how they had coped with a recent crisis. They were asked a number of questions including whether they had consulted friends about the problem and whether they had drawn on knowledge from a similar problem in the past.

RESULTS Both husbands and wives used more problem-focused than emotion-focused strategies, but wives reported using emotion-focused ways more than their husbands did. Higher-income and better-educated participants were more likely to report using problem-focused methods, although all participants reported greater use of emotion-focused strategies when coping with highly stressful events such as bereavement.

CONCLUSION Use of emotion-focused and problem-focused strategies varies according to gender, background and the type of event being experienced.

In an important paper for the history of health psychology, Folkman *et al.* (1986) set out eight types of coping strategy employed by individuals facing stress. Of the eight strategies they identified, two are problem-focused, five are emotion-focused and one could be seen as either. Folkman *et al.*'s types are set out below.

PROBLEM-FOCUSED APPROACHES

1. **Planful problem-solving** is a rather obvious strategy. It is about planning a way out of a problem. While it may seem to many to be the first step when a person is in trouble, a lot of people simply do not use this approach, preferring instead to avoid problems or expect fate or their god to help them.

2. **Confronting** involves dealing with the problem or the source of the problem 'head on'. If the bank is threatening to foreclose a loan, speaking to the bank manager, rather than drinking to forget or keeping feelings secret, is a sensible form of confronting. Do not mistake 'confronting' for 'confrontation' or aggression; not all confronting is aggressive, although much of it can be.

EMOTION-FOCUSED APPROACHES

3. **Escape avoidance,** just as the term suggests, involves 'escapism'. The person tries to avoid the problem by thinking about other things, or by drinking alcohol 'to forget', or by having unrealistic fantasies about magical or lucky ways out of the situation. The person who has been made redundant and is about to lose their house because they have been unable to pay the mortgage may decide that they feel happier when drunk, or they may spend time daydreaming about being offered a great job or about winning the lottery. Another common avoidance strategy is to 'throw oneself into one's work'.

4. **Distancing** involves putting the problem at a metaphorical distance, which can be achieved in a number of ways. Humour is one approach: making the problem into a joke. Another is essentially **denial**, trying not to think about the problem, as if it hadn't happened.

5. **Positive reappraisal** is about finding some good in the bad. Experiences are cognitively re-framed so that the positive in them is identified and focused on. Therefore, people say things like 'losing my sight has done me good because I have put my life into perspective' or 'without losing my baby I would not have realised that other people needed my help and started to work for a charity'.

6. **Self-controlling,** as you would expect, involves keeping feelings controlled internally, without seeking external help. It can involve 'bottling up' feelings rather than sharing them, and not showing others that stress is being experienced.

7. **Accepting responsibility** is, in many ways, a healthy approach – it can be beneficial to accept responsibility for one's actions, and therefore one's problems. Many problems are brought on by a person's own thoughts and actions. However, not all are, and sometimes we are simply unlucky or the victims of the actions of others. Accepting responsibility is not a good strategy, however, when a person is not actually responsible. In these circumstances it is likely to engender negative feelings and affect self-esteem.

8. **Seeking social support** is about sharing problems. In contrast with the person who 'bottles up', others prefer to 'get things off their chest'. Thus, seeking social support is a crucial coping strategy for many people. They want to tell others about their problems, because it makes them feel better. The saying 'a problem shared is a problem halved' illustrates this approach.

Seeking social support is unusual in that it can be *both* emotion-focused (in that it is about sharing feelings) *and* problem-focused (in that it is a way of getting advice about dealing with the problem).

Most coping behaviour falls into one or more of these categories. They are not exclusive. Because a person uses one strategy does not mean that they will not use others, even when strategies may give rise to contradictory thoughts or ideas. Therefore, a stressor may lead to a combination of coping strategies being employed – sometimes confronting, sometimes escape-avoidant. Because someone wants to face a problem today does not mean they will choose to do the same tomorrow: tomorrow they may prefer to hide away from it by going on holiday or working a long day.

Another important consideration is the fact that different stressors may require different approaches, and a person who typically uses a restricted range of strategies may have difficulties coping with a stressor not experienced before. The planful, accepting-responsibility or confrontative strategies are particularly useful when a person can actually *do* something about the problem. If they are stressed by noisy neighbours, for instance, there are social and, ultimately, legal ways to deal with this. However, such strategies might be less useful when a person is powerless to change or affect the stressor. If someone loses a leg due to bone cancer they are unlikely to be able to accept responsibility for it themselves, may have no one to confront, and certainly cannot make plans that will change the fact that they have lost a leg. Admittedly, they can plan for the future and work on living a full life from this moment on, but the fact that the leg has been lost remains. In such a case, seeking social support, positive appraisal and distancing via humour might be more appropriate techniques of coping.

EVALUATIVE COMMENT

Sometimes one action or behaviour can be seen as an example of more than one type of coping strategy, calling Folkman *et al.*'s (1986) categories into question. For example, people who are diagnosed with an illness sometimes become fascinated by their illness and read up on it. They become an expert on the subject and perhaps are able to give advice to others. They may work for or establish some self-help group or charity. This behaviour is known as intellectualisation of the illness.

Looking at Folkman *et al.*'s (1986) division into types of strategy, intellectualisation seems to span more than one of them. It is clearly a distancing approach, looking at the illness as a thing 'out there' to be studied, rather than a property of the person. It is also, perhaps, positive reappraisal, since becoming an expert on an illness is not perceived as a negative thing at all. It might also be confrontive coping, because the person is dealing with the issue head on and, perhaps, confronting others to fight for rights, research monies, and so on. Ultimately, this approach could also be seen as long-term planning. If a person seeks to help others (and themselves) through research and knowledge, this is a planful strategy. In addition, social support is sought and perhaps set up via this mode of action, especially if the individual establishes or attends self-help groups and, perhaps, taps into these for purposes of research. The person who tackles the illness in this way also accepts responsibility: they might be seen as saying 'if anyone ought to try to help people with this illness, I as a sufferer should' and 'if you want something doing, do it yourself'.

Approach/avoidance conflicts and strategies

Where stress originates from within the person this is often because of internal conflict due to competing motives. For example, if a person has to choose between two options for a university course, the dilemma of the choice creates a conflict that may become a major source of stress and anxiety. Sarafino (1994) identified two opposing tendencies that arise from this type of stress: approach and avoidance. These tendencies can result in three types of conflict.

1. Approach/approach conflict occurs where there are two equally desirable but incompatible options. For example, where a person wants to have a fit, healthy body but also wants to eat delicious but fattening foods.

2. Avoidance/avoidance conflict occurs where there are two equally undesirable options. For example, when a patient with a serious illness is faced with the option of having a traumatic operation or undergoing long-term therapy with unpleasant side-effects.

3. Approach/avoidance conflict occurs where there are desirable and undesirable factors within a single option. For example, where a person wants to go to the gym to exercise regularly but believes that gym membership is an unnecessary and extravagant expense.

Such conflicts can be very difficult to resolve, not least because of the consequences of making what might turn out to be the 'wrong' choice.

PRACTICAL Activity

Write down your own example of:

• an approach/approach conflict

• an avoidance/avoidance conflict

• an approach/avoidance conflict.

Consider the type and amount of stress each conflict you have identified might cause.

Roth and Cohen (1986) have explained approach and avoidance as ways of coping with stress, making a distinction between activity directed towards the source of stress (approach) and activity directed away from the source of stress (avoidance). According to Roth and Cohen (1986) people have a natural tendency to use different coping styles, which affects how they perceive and respond to potentially stressful situations. Approachers, or sensitisers, actively seek out information about possible harmful or stressful events such as flu epidemics or conditions such as hypertension. Avoiders or repressors selectively avoid such information and forget whatever they have heard or read about potentially harmful or stressful events.

Approachers typically show high external anxiety but low physiological arousal when faced with a stressful event, whereas avoiders typically show low external anxiety but high physiological arousal as a response to stress.

Study 4.6

AIM Field *et al.* (1988) investigated the effects of using approach and avoidance strategies in a hospital setting.

METHOD Children in hospital to undergo surgical procedures were observed for certain types of behaviour and categorised as either sensitisers (approachers) or repressors (avoiders). Sensitiser children (approachers) asked more questions, made more protests and observed what was happening to them as procedures were being carried out. Repressor children (avoiders) asked few questions, protested less frequently and shied away from procedures, seemingly pretending that they were not happening.

RESULTS The sensitiser children who took more interest in the procedures and were more sensitive to their treatment made quicker recoveries than those who attempted to avoid the stress and pretend it was not happening.

CONCLUSION It appears that while confronting a problem by approaching it directly may be stressful at the time, it may, in the long run, be more beneficial than avoidance.

Suls and Fletcher (1985) carried out a meta-analysis of results from a large number of studies and came to two conclusions. First, avoidance strategies benefit coping in the short-term – for example, when first diagnosed with a serious illness it might be better to at least partly deny what is happening. Second, they found that approach strategies are more effective for long-term coping, which usually requires some form of planning, decision-making and action to deal with the source of the stress.

Defence mechanisms and stress

Freud suggested that we use unconscious coping mechanisms to help us deal with the stresses and strains of life, essentially by avoiding or somehow minimising the stressful event. Defence mechanisms act to defend us against reality by either denying that stressful events are happening or distorting them so as to make them seem less harmful. Intellectualisation is one example of how defence mechanisms might be used to help cope with stress. Other defence mechanisms are outlined in Figure 4.3.

EVALUATIVE COMMENT
While most defence mechanisms are usually seen as pure avoidance and therefore deemed to be rather negative ways of coping with stress, some of them can be seen as helpful and constructive. Suppression, sublimation, anticipation and altruism might be seen as positive and useful examples of defence mechanisms whereas repression, denial, projection and displacement might be seen as negative and unproductive.

Defence mechanism	How it might be used to cope with stress
Repression	Anxiety-provoking thoughts are kept from the conscious mind. A person might never consciously think about how many relatives have had a certain type of cancer.
Suppression	Making a conscious effort not to think about stressful things – as, for example, when waiting for the results of examinations.
Displacement	Anger and frustration about a stressor is taken out on something else – for example, where a sick person might shout at those caring for them.
Sublimation	Energy is redirected from an unacceptable goal to an acceptable one. A person who has been diagnosed with a serious illness might channel their energies into writing about experiences of the illness.
Projection	Unconsciously believing that one's own problem is actually someone else's. For example, an alcoholic might believe that a friend has a drink problem when, in fact, it is he who has a problem.
Altruism	A healthy defence mechanism whereby a stressed person might help others as a way of coping with their own problem. Many voluntary organisations are run by individuals who have had similar stressful experiences in the past.
Denial	One way of dealing with unpleasant events is to deny they are happening. So, a woman might deny that her husband has left her because to consciously accept that it has happened would be too much to cope with.

Figure 4.3: Defence mechanisms used to cope with stress

Other coping strategies

Aside from the three categories of coping strategies already considered, Nolen-Hoeksema *et al.* (1997) identified two other classifications of coping, this time clearly based in the personalities of the individuals themselves and linked to **rumination**. Copers can be ruminators or non-ruminators. In their study of people who had experienced the death of a partner, they found that some people tended to 'chew over' (hence 'ruminate') their grief without achieving anything. They would comment on their thoughts and feelings, repeating stressful assertions without really dealing with them in any way, almost as if describing someone else's thoughts rather than their own. Ruminators, typically, will repeat phrases such as 'I'm not a lucky person', 'I feel terrible', 'I can't seem to get right', 'I don't get better', 'it seems unfair' without really trying to find answers for the questions they generate. In contrast, non-ruminators create plans for dealing with their problems, and work through difficulties with a view to changing things. Ruminators are more likely to experience longer periods of depression or grief following the loss of a partner.

REFLECTIVE Activity

Would you regard yourself as a ruminator or a non-ruminator? What about members of your family? Think about each in turn, and classify them if you can. Then reflect on whether you think that rumination is something that children might learn from their families, or whether it could be inherited. In addition, consider whether the ruminator/non-ruminator distinction is helpful. For example, is it the case that a person might change their strategy depending on their circumstances and the nature of the stress they face?

EVALUATIVE COMMENT

Stress is a fact of life for many health professionals, and the coping mechanisms that apply to their patients also apply to them. Medical students and doctors have been known to make jokes about disease and death, which some people would regard as highly distasteful. By doing this, they are using distance coping. The health professions, like many others, are high-stress occupations. Chronic stress in those professions that have a high level of contact with clients (teaching, law, policing, medicine, etc.) can have some particularly strange effects on the person, effects that are collectively referred to as *burnout*. The term was coined by Freudenberger (1974), and has since been used extensively to describe the physical and emotional changes that can occur when job stress forces an individual to adapt to their environment.

The three main characteristics of burnout, according to Maslach (1982) are: *depersonalisation* (ceasing to care for and have feelings for other people); *emotional exhaustion* (simply feeling tired of things, and unable to muster up the resources to be an emotional being); *perceived inadequacy* (feeling unable to do one's job properly). If you watch modern TV dramas about doctors and nurses, you will be able to identify instances where characters have experienced burnout.

4.3 Managing stress

Behavioural and cognitive approaches

In addition to the very real and significant ways in which social support can moderate stress, literally thousands of ways of reducing stress are available. Some of these are more unusual and 'wacky' than others, but most can be classified into the ways in which they effect their stress relief. The main classification is into *behavioural* and *cognitive* approaches. Behavioural approaches aim to change behaviour in a way that will help to reduce stress, even if only indirectly. They work on the level of our actions. Cognitive approaches aim to help us to see stress and stressful incidents in a different way, to recode them as things that are not really stressful at all. They work on the level of our thoughts. As you might expect, some techniques for reducing and managing stress are a mixture of the two.

Exercise is one way to relieve stress. It is a behavioural method, since all it involves is getting people to change their behaviour and do some exercise! Studies have shown a relationship between the ability of the body to cope with stress and indulgence in exercise, especially aerobic exercise. Sinyor *et al.* (1983) compared hormonal reactions to an artificial stressor in people who exercise regularly and people who do not. They found that the exercisers had better rates of recovery from the stress. Imagine driving a car up a hill. The engine has to do more work than on the flat. The hill represents stress for the machine. A well-serviced vehicle will be more likely to get you up the hill than an 'old banger'. By the same token, if you look after your body, it will look after you when you need it.

Relaxation is another path to reducing stress, achieved commonly through things such as meditation. Relaxation is an example of a mixed technique. It is behavioural in that people are expected to actually do something physically, even if it is just to sit still compared to how they normally buzz around. However, it is also cognitive in that you are also expected to do something with your mind. In the case of meditation, you are often trying to concentrate very hard on nothing at all, or on a very simple object or sound. You are directing your thoughts.

In Japanese offices, staff are often encouraged to exercise at work, and calming sounds such as that of rain are played through the company public address system. Reducing stress, therefore, is not just a private, individual thing – it can be a public or group activity. In China, early morning *t'ai chi* sessions are to be seen in open-air, public squares (see page 116).

BIOFEEDBACK

Scientific involvement in relaxation-based stress reduction has, at times, centred around the issue of **biofeedback**. Biofeedback involves wiring up a person to measure their vital signs, such as heart rate and blood pressure, and enabling them to monitor these signs so they can control them consciously. By learning to lower blood pressure or heart rate, the individual can relax more effectively and take control over bodily functions that have a central role in health. We all have control over some bodily processes which we normally regard as involuntary. We don't have to think about breathing, but when we want to we can change our breathing patterns. The same applies to walking or blinking. There are some things, however, that it is harder to change, although it is still possible. Heart rate can be consciously reduced, or increased, but normally this requires training. Luria (1958) is famous for his studies of a man with an astonishing memory. It is less well known that the same man also had an unusual ability to alter his heart rate quite dramatically, and to change the temperature of different parts of his body, so that, for instance, one hand was hotter than the other.

In China, early morning *t'ai chi* sessions take place in public squares – a good way of avoiding stress!

EVALUATIVE COMMENT

The literature on biofeedback is very mixed. Many researchers find that it does not work, many that it does. When it does work for a person, it can be used to help with a range of health problems, not just stress but also anxiety, hypertension, headache and other pain (Gatchel *et al.*, 1989). Notice that each of these health problems leads to stress and is also a product of stress. The main problem with biofeedback is that it involves reducing stress signs during periods of non-stress. A person learns the techniques when sitting in a laboratory or office, comfortable, warm and generally quite relaxed. In real life, stress usually occurs in circumstances that do not resemble this. This means that the skill of reducing heart rate or pain does not necessarily generalise to times when the stressors are actually present (Holmes, 1984).

Rational emotive behaviour therapy is a cognitive approach based on the work of Ellis (1962), who argued that a lot of problems in life are due to the way that people think about themselves and events; by changing the thoughts, we can change the stressor. For example, some people adopt a catastrophising approach to problems.

Catastrophisers are people who exaggerate problems, and generally think that the world is almost about to end every time something goes wrong. Most of us have met someone who behaves like this from time to time, and many of us do have less dramatic faulty cognitions that contribute to our stress. Furthermore, we are more likely to think unhelpful thoughts when we are in the presence of a set of stressors, rather than just one. When something goes wrong on an otherwise normal day we can often cope. But when it happens on a day when other things have gone wrong, and we are tired and hungry and upset, then we are even more likely to reach a point close to catastrophising. The tendency to catastrophise shows itself in phrases like 'the last straw' and 'that's just about put the tin hat on it!'.

Rational-emotive therapies seek to deal with emotional responses to problems by replacing them with more positive and rational ideas instead. Figure 4.4 shows the kind of thoughts a person may have about something going wrong, and the type of response therapists would aim to make them have instead.

Faulty cognition (emotional response)	Healthy cognition (rational response)
Oh no, it's all spoiled now.	One thing has gone wrong. One is not all.
There's no point.	There is always some point.
I'm sick of it all.	I'm sick of this particular thing.
Everyone hates me.	Some people dislike me, but most like me.
Why is it always like this?	It isn't always like this.
It always happens to me.	This kind of thing happens to everyone now and then.
I am jinxed.	Everyone is unlucky sometimes.

Figure 4.4: The work of a rational-emotive behaviour therapist involves replacing faulty thoughts with more rational ones

Over time, rational-emotive therapy has developed into the more general cognitive-behavioural therapy now commonly used by clinical psychologists dealing with a range of clients with mental health difficulties involving ill-health, stress and anxiety.

Systematic desensitisation is another behavioural technique that can be applied to stress. It has been developed from the early work of Wolpe (1958) and works as follows. When you first put your clothes on, you feel them against your body. After a short while, you seem not to notice them any more. Similarly, when you buy a new clock, you hear it ticking. Eventually, you hardly ever hear it. This occurs because our nervous system adapts to stimuli in the environment. If it didn't, we would be driven crazy by the bombardment of sights, sounds, smells, and so on, all around us all of the time. Wolpe believed that we could capitalise on this property of the nervous system. If someone has a negative reaction to something, we simply get them used to the thing they don't like, and eventually they won't mind it. This is the idea of desensitisation. The systematic part comes in because it is not feasible to get people used to something they hate straight away. It has to be done bit by bit – that is, systematically. It is the way in which most phobias are treated today, with a very high level of success. Figure 4.5 shows the process in treating a phobia.

Just as it is possible to treat a phobia with this gradual method of exposure, so we can also treat stress by gradual exposure to the stressor. For example, if a person is habitually stressed by minor hassles, exposure to individual minor hassles, one at a time, will slowly teach the person that they can really cope with them.

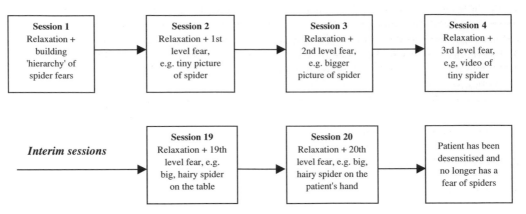

Figure 4.5: Systematic desensitisation of a fear of spiders

PRACTICAL Activity

Imagine a person has a fear of public speaking. Make a list of 20 separate stages you could use in systematic desensitisation to cure this. (It is difficult, but possible.)

Other approaches

HYPNOSIS

Hypnosis shares some of its characteristics with relaxation and meditation. A person who is hypnotised is in what seems to be a highly relaxed state. What makes hypnosis different is that the client is extremely sensitive to suggestion. While hypnotised, they can be told to behave in certain ways that can persist when they are brought out of the hypnotic state. This state is thought to be a direct line to the subconscious. When the client comes back to normality they do not remember the instructions given by the hypnotherapist, but they seem to be able to follow them in their waking lives.

Anything that can change behaviour has the capacity to change a person's health, and hypnosis is very commonly used to help people stop smoking and lose weight by changing their eating habits. Modern dentists are starting to show some good applications of hypnosis as a substitute for anaesthetic during painful procedures. With respect to stress, hypnosis may or may not have some effects, and it is important to remember that only a proportion of people are susceptible to hypnotic suggestion. If you are one of the people who are not, it is nothing other than a waste of time. If you can be hypnotised, what little evidence there is simply suggests that hypnosis can reduce stress, but no better than other techniques that involve relaxation (Wadden and Anderton, 1982).

Gruzelier, Levy, Williams and Henderson (2001) looked at self-hypnosis as a means of reducing examination stress in a sample of 22 medical students. The participants were asked to think, during hypnosis or being relaxed, about their immune system, using imagery. They found that biochemical measures of stress were reduced in students using immune-related imagery, and that they reported fewer symptoms of viral infection during the examination period under study.

AUTOGENIC TRAINING

Autogenic training is, in some ways, a development of relaxation training and also hypnosis, mainly involving self-hypnosis. About 100 years ago, Dr Johannes Schulz, a German

psychiatrist, started to develop his ideas about individuals being able to calm themselves and lower their blood pressure, heart rate and other physical signs of stress. The aim is to reduce the fight-or-flight response described elsewhere in this chapter. Through the initial involvement of a therapist, people are taught to focus on specific parts of their body and to have effects on them while they are in a concentrated state of consciousness quite similar to when people are able to hypnotise themselves.

The six key features of the technique involve the person thinking through stages something like this:

1. my arms and legs feel heavy

2. my arms and legs feel warm

3. my heart feels warm and heavy

4. my breathing is slow and calm

5. my stomach feels warm

6. my forehead feels cool.

Each exercise is practised before moving on to the next, and the learning process can take weeks. Eventually the individual is able to relax themselves through this method quickly and efficiently, and without help from anyone else.

EVALUATIVE COMMENT

Those who are involved in autogenic training claim great successes from it, but one must remember that they also stand to profit from any successes they report. The research literature on autogenic training is very mixed, and there are few properly controlled and *randomised controlled trials* of this technique available. Those that do exist seem to suggest that autogenic training can work, but that its effects are no better than those obtained from other relaxation and meditation approaches. It is fair to say that autogenic training is extremely unlikely to do a person any harm and could do some good, so it is not to be ignored. In fact, in the UK, doctors can prescribe a course of autogenic training through the National Health Service for people who are likely to benefit from it, such as those with hypertension or moderate, clinical levels of anxiety.

TIME MANAGEMENT

Time management is a common technique aimed at reducing stress indirectly, by eliminating the feelings of being under time pressures. In the business world there are expert consultants in time management who can demand high fees for teaching people how to manage their time effectively. Companies realise that an employee who manages time well gets more work done in the time available and is also less stressed. Less stress equates directly to better health and this means fewer days off work. Stress is estimated to result in millions of lost days of work per year in most developed countries. Aside from the official statistics on this, there are also the unofficial cases. When some people pretend to be physically ill because they cannot face going in to work, it is likely to be stress that is putting them into that position.

Time management can be achieved relatively easily, if you have the time for it! Indeed, many people fail to manage time effectively because they fail to find time to set about managing time. Time-management techniques can be picked up from little books at little cost, or someone can invest in very expensive, individually tailored programmes from a 'personal trainer'. Either way, well-managed time can mean a healthy person.

SOCIAL SUPPORT ENHANCEMENT

Social support enhancement is a key factor in cutting down on the damaging effects of stress. It is not always easy to do, simply because it is often painfully difficult for people to make friends. However, by joining clubs and 'getting out more', people who are lonely may find ways to generate more social support, which as we have seen can have a significant impact on their health, even their likely age of death. Additionally, TV campaigns such as those in the UK, asking people to check on their neighbours regularly, especially if they are old and live alone, may assist in this. The purpose of such a request goes beyond personal safety, and can easily contribute to psychological health.

CONTROL ENHANCEMENT

Control enhancement is another issue that is achieved by a range of techniques. We have already identified that stress is something that can be moderated by perceived control over situations. By altering perceived control, we can make a difference to perceived stress. First, control can be increased in real terms – for example, where employers allow employees to make decisions and control their working practices within reason. Second, cognitive behavioural techniques are a good method, involving changing people's perceptions of themselves and their sense of control. By a range of methods, usually involving some kind of more or less sophisticated conditioning, people learn to think differently.

STRESS INOCULATION TRAINING

Stress inoculation training (Meichenbaum and Deffenbacher, 1988) is a specific form of stress management, based on cognitive behaviour therapy. It involves training people in new skills, through three phases: conceptualisation, skills acquisition, and rehearsal and application. In the conceptualisation phase, people are taught what the body does as a reaction to stress, and what the common psychological consequences are. They are made to analyse their own reactions to stress. In the skills acquisition and rehearsal phase, people are asked to try out alternative reactions. So instead of waiting in a queue provoking the usual thoughts of 'Come on, come on, hurry up, come on, I haven't got all day ...', the person is encouraged to think something like 'Keep calm ... the queue will go down in time ... my anxiousness will not make a difference to the queue.' They are taught techniques of stress reduction such as relaxation, and positive coping styles are emphasised. In the application phase, people have to really try these things out in their lives, keeping records to see the differences they make to them. This is, in essence, an extended form of cognitive behavioural therapy, which has been shown to help stressed individuals with a moderate degree of success.

EVALUATIVE COMMENT

Stress is complicated and depends on factors both inside and outside the individual. Stress is a problem for us all. It represents one of the more easily demonstrable cases of a link between the body and the mind, and as such it is something that a professional health psychologist needs to be able to do something about. In some ways, as we learn more about stress, combating it becomes more difficult. Not only does it become more complicated, but also the nature of stress changes as the world keeps on changing. A consequence of the modern world is higher levels of perceived stress. With every time-saving device comes a new stressor. Computers are great because they do things quickly, but we rant and rave when they crash. Mobile telephones can save lives, time and trouble, but also create stress if we are worried that they might cause ill-health, or when we would rather be out of the reach of others in order to have time to ourselves. We keep on finding new ways to become stressed. We are, therefore, unlikely to eliminate stress for good.

4.4 Sample questions

SAMPLE QUESTION

(a)   Using an example, explain what is meant by a problem-focused approach to coping with stress.
      (AO1 = 2, AO2 = 2)   *(4 marks)*

(b)   Outline what is meant by a defence mechanism and suggest how one named defence mechanism
      might be used to cope with stress.
      (AO1 = 3, AO2 = 1)   *(4 marks)*

(c)   Describe and discuss the behavioural approach to managing stress.
      (AO1 = 5, AO2 = 7)   *(12 marks)*

QUESTIONS, ANSWERS AND COMMENTS

(a)   Outline one physiological technique for measuring stress.
      (AO1 = 3)   *(3 marks)*

(b)   Outline and briefly discuss the use of self-report techniques for the measurement of stress.
      (AO1 = 2, AO2 = 3)   *(5 marks)*

(c)   Discuss the role of personal variables in mediating response to stress.
      (AO1 = 5, AO2 = 7)   *(12 marks)*

Answer to (a)

One technique for measuring stress that is physiological is to take blood or urine and test it to see what hormones levels are present. If a person is stressed blood contains substances like catecholamines (norepinephrine) and extra corticosteroids.

Comment: This answer gets the full three marks.

Answer to (b)

Self-report measures are usually questionnaires like the 'daily hassles scale' (Kanner) and the SSRI developed by Holmes and Rahe. The Holmes and Rahe scale looks at how many stressful events a person has experienced in the last year. This can then be used to see how stressed they are. The trouble with these types of scale is that people might not be honest or may forget exactly what has happened. It is also difficult to say that a particular event has a certain value. Why, for example, does pregnancy always rate 40? It might be a child that is wanted or it might be not wanted at all. Then the stress would be different. Also what is meant by 'change in eating habits'? Some items are not that objectively defined.

Comment: This is an example of a full five-mark answer. Here the candidate shows a good knowledge of two self-report methods and provides some elaboration of the SSRI. The description is followed by general limitations of self-report and by specific problems of the SSRI.

Answer to (c)

Several personal variables might mediate the effect of stress. Here we shall examine the effect of having a Type A personality and the effect of locus of control.

A Type A personality, as identified by Friedman and Rosenman (1959), shows certain types of responses including competitiveness and drive to succeed, time pressure and anger or hostility. These people can

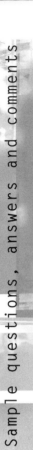

be identified using an interview procedure. This type of person is more likely to react physiologically to stress (reactivity), and is more likely to suffer from stress-related disease, especially cardiovascular problems like heart disease. One difficulty with the Type A classification is that it is not clear whether Type A is inherited or not, or whether Type A people can change. Certainly there is a lot of evidence to show that Type A people respond differently to stressful situations as their heart rate increases much more than that of controls. It seems, therefore, that Friedman and Rosenman identified a key factor in how we deal with stress. It seems it is easier for Type B people to cope than it is for Type A. In the original study they compared the lifestyles etc. of Types A and B, and found that Type As were more likely to have heart disease in their family, and work harder and be more active than Type Bs.

Another factor mediating the effect of stress could be locus of control (Rotter, 1966). If we have an external locus of control it means we feel that we cannot control what happens to us. However, if we have an internal locus of control it means we feel we can have some influence over what happens to us. Obviously external people feel more stressed when bad things happen because they feel there is nothing they can do about it. Frankenhaeuser's study of sawmill workers found that where people have no control over the work aspect of their lives they show high levels of physiological stress. Knowing that a sense of control is important for combating the effects of stress can be used to help people. For example, in a stressful situation, such as a prison environment, prisoners could be given some measure of control, perhaps by deciding when they have exercise times or what they have to eat. The opposite of control is helplessness, which was shown in famous studies of learned helplessness to have highly negative effects on stress experienced by dogs who could not escape from electric shocks.

In summary, it seems that a Type A person with an external locus of control would respond to stress much more negatively than a Type B person with an internal locus of control. It would be interesting to know whether there is any relationship between Type A/B and locus of control. Finally we must remember that, although personality type and locus of control might to some degree affect how we deal with stress, other factors, such as hardiness, might also be important.

Comment: Here the candidate correctly identifies and describes two personal variables and explains how they might mediate the effects of stress. Perhaps a little more could have been said about Type B, but there is sufficient descriptive information for the full five AO1 marks. There are several analytical points in the answer and the evidence presented is reasonably well applied in evaluation. Note how the candidate's understanding of the material is demonstrated in the attempt to apply knowledge to a real-life situation. The answer could possibly have been a bit more detailed or have included a little more evaluation but it is definitely worthy of marks in the top band. The full five marks are awarded for AO1 and four for AO2, out of the seven available.

4.5 FURTHER READING

Introductory texts

Curtis, A.J. 2000: **Health Psychology.** Routledge, London

Eysenck, M. (ed.) 1998: **Psychology, an Integrated Approach.** Longman, London

Gross, R.D. 2001: **Psychology, the Science of Mind and Behaviour**. 4th Ed. Hodder & Stoughton, London

Gross, R. and McIlveen, R. 1998: **Psychology, a New Introduction.** Hodder and Stoughton, London

Harari, P. and Legge, K. 2001: **Psychology and Health.** Heinemann, London

Specialist sources

Forshaw, M. 2002b: **Essential Health Psychology.** Arnold, London

Ogden, J. 2000: **Health Psychology: A Textbook**. 2nd Ed. Open University Press, Buckingham

Sarafino, E.P. 1998: **Health Psychology, Biopsychosocial Interactions**. 3rd Ed. Wiley, Oxford

Sheridan, C.L. and Radmacher, S.A. 1992: **Health Psychology.** Wiley, Chichester

Glossary

This glossary is meant as a quick guide to some of the terms used in this book. It does not provide foolproof and exact definitions of the terms, since in most cases exact definitions are almost impossible to give in a few words.

Active placebo A placebo that mimics the effects of a therapeutic drug, i.e. has side-effects without the therapeutic effects.

Adherence A term used to denote how a patient 'sticks to' medical advice. This term is, today, used instead of *compliance*.

Analgesia Pain relief, which can be effected physically, using chemicals, or psychologically, using cognitive techniques or hypnosis.

Appraisal support When a stressed person is encouraged or enabled to evaluate their own state of health and are thus able to put their *stressors* into context; appraisal support is the name given to this.

Aversion therapy A therapeutic process whereby people are 'put off' doing things by associating them with unpleasant sensations or thoughts. To stop someone eating chocolate, aversion therapy might involve giving people chocolate flavoured with a bitter substance.

Biofeedback A form of therapeutic process through which people can learn to alter their physiological processes by watching them change on some kind of 'meter'. For instance, relaxation can be taught by showing a person the physiological indicators of relaxation and training them to control their bodily responses to create a relaxed state.

Biopsychosocial model The prevailing model of health within health psychology. The focus is on the interaction of the mind and the body, and there is an acceptance of the range of individual differences in personality and culture that can affect health. More consideration is given to how the life of an individual is affected by their illness, and vice versa.

Buffering hypothesis/direct hypothesis These are hypotheses about how social support brings about reductions in stress. In the direct hypothesis, social support is directly good for you, whereas in the buffering hypothesis social support acts as a buffer, cushioning the individual against major *stressors* but having little impact on minor hassles.

Burnout A term used to describe the syndrome affecting people who have experienced stress and fatigue in their work over a long period of time. It is characterised by lack of empathy for others, loss of perceived self-efficacy, and exhaustion.

Central nervous system Essentially, the brain and spinal cord.

Chronic illness Any illness that is likely to last a long time or a lifetime. It is contrasted with acute illness.

Cognitive dissonance A feeling experienced when there is some degree of contradiction between two outcomes. When a person does something for themselves that also harms them in some way, cognitive dissonance is felt. For example, if a person spends a lot of money on a holiday, they might harm themselves by creating financial difficulties. In order to reduce cognitive dissonance, they must believe that it was 'worth it', that they have benefited from the holiday and that it has been good for their health.

Complementary medicine Also known as alternative medicine. Health practices and systems like reflexology and homeopathy that are suppposed to heal using mechanisms other than those used by orthodox medicine. Doctors prefer the term 'complementary' medicine, since 'alternative' implies that orthodox medicine is not required at all.

Compliance/non-compliance The extent to which a person adheres to medical advice and/or a treatment regimen. The term is now ill-favoured, and *adherence* is mainly used instead.

Conditioning This refers to the pairing up of actions and their reactions. Pavlov first demonstrated this by showing that if a dog learned to associate the ringing of a bell with food, the bell alone would produce salivation after a number of such pairings.

Confronting This is a *coping* strategy that involves dealing with a problem by facing it and by arguing out problems with people.

Contingency contracting A form of reward system used in therapies such as cognitive behavioural therapy. The client enters into a contract with the therapist, which means that certain things will be given or withdrawn depending on the client's behaviour.

Coping A significant term in health psychology, it is used in a range of contexts, none of which is at odds with the normal dictionary definition of coping.

Demand characteristics The perceived demand upon an individual taking part in a study. What a person perceives as the purpose of a study can affect how they behave or answer the questions they are asked.

Denial A refusal to accept that a health problem exists. A common *coping* strategy.

Depersonalisation Viewing others as if they are not thinking, feeling people but rather objects or units of production. This is a characteristic of *burnout*.

Direct hypothesis See *Buffering hypothesis*.

Distancing A form of *coping* with a problem or *stressor* in which a person distances the problem from themselves, perhaps by laughing about it.

Emotion-focused coping Contrasted with *problem-focused coping*, this involves addressing and working through one's emotional reaction to a problem rather than dealing with solving the problem itself.

Emotional support A form of social support that, as its name suggests, refers to being loved, cared for and listened to.

Endocrine system The hormone-producing glands of the body that are responsible for regulating many of the body's mechanisms, such as thirst.

Escape avoidance Coping with a problem by avoiding it. This is classic escapism such as 'drinking to forget' or 'throwing oneself into one's work'.

Esteem support Social support that takes the form of others showing an individual that they are valued and respected.

Eustress Positive stress, which may be good for the individual. Some people appear to thrive on moderately stressful situations. In addition, the exhilaration felt from watching a horror movie, or riding a rollercoaster is similar to the feelings experienced during acute stress, although the context is all-important in determining the way the situation is perceived.

Fight-or-flight response A physiological response to an environmental threat. When in danger, the body becomes biologically prepared to either stand and fight or to run away.

Fighting spirit A term used to describe a personality characteristic that, some evidence suggests, might enable a person to defeat certain illnesses.

Gate-control theory A theory of pain perception that takes into account the many physical and psychological dimensions of pain, and likens the movement of pain signals to the brain to objects passing through a gate of adjustable size.

Hardiness A personality characteristic that may predispose people to being more resilient to disease and illness.

Hassles scale A stress-measurement scale intended to detect stresses caused by minor hassles as opposed to major life problems.

Health action process approach A multifactorial model of health behaviours taking into account motivation, self-efficacy and personal will.

Health belief model (HBM) A model that helps to predict health behaviours based upon perceptions of susceptibility to an illness, costs and benefits of the health behaviour, and environmental 'cues to action' that can trigger the behaviour.

Health beliefs A term used to denote the thoughts and folk knowledge a person may have about health. For example, a person may believe that one glass of brandy a day promotes good health.

Homeopathy A complementary therapy involving the consumption of 'tinctures' of plant extracts, which are heavily diluted with water, often to the point where no molecules of the original substance are present in the therapy. Homeopathic therapists argue that the substance leaves a molecular impression on the water molecules, which can have a therapeutic effect.

Hostility A characteristic associated with *Type A personality* behaviour.

Hypochondriasis An unhealthy, sometimes disabling, preoccupation with ill-health, where a person believes themselves to be suffering from one or a number of illnesses or diseases when there is no medical evidence that they are.

Illness cognitions A term used to denote the thoughts and folk knowledge that a person may have about illness. For example, the beliefs that cancer can be contagious or that the mind can cure the body.

Immunocompetence The general health and efficiency of the immune system.

Informational support Support provided by information – such as books, leaflets, the Internet – or by knowledgeable individuals and experts.

Instrumental support Practical support, such as financial backing or gifts of material goods.

Intellectualisation A *coping* mechanism in illness, whereby people distance their illness from themselves by studying it and speaking of it as an academic, rather than personal, phenomenon.

Locus of control A term used to describe the way in which people ascribe the things that happen to them as being either their own doing (internal locus of control) or the doings of others (external). External locus of control is divided into powerful others and chance (fate).

Medical model An outmoded view of the human condition that has been persistent in medicine for most of its history and is still present in some spheres today. Essentially, the human being is seen as almost entirely reducible to tissues and physiological processes, and the culture, thoughts and beliefs of a person are generally ignored.

Medicalisation A term used mainly by sociologists to describe how the medical profession may have 'taken over' certain aspects of normal life, such as childbirth.

Meta-analysis A form of analysis of the results of experiments, which involves adding together various results from similar studies as if they were all part of one bigger study.

Non-compliance See *Compliance*.

Obesity Being overweight, commonly defined technically as having a body mass index greater than 25. This is computed as weight in kilograms divided by height in metres.

Palliative care The branch of medicine devoted to supporting people who are deemed terminally ill.

Peripheral nervous system All aspects of the nervous system excluding the *central nervous system*.

Placebo A substance that is inert but is given to a patient who believes that it has therapeutic properties.

Planful problem-solving A strategy for *coping* that involves planning a way out of a problem state.

Positive reappraisal Turning a problem into something positive by looking for ways in which a *stressor* has benefited the individual.

Positivism A view, attached to *reductionism* and the *medical model*, that there are indisputable 'facts' that are 'out there' for us to discover.

Problem-focused coping Contrasted with *emotion-focused coping*, this involves dealing with a problem by working through it and seeking practical solutions.

Psychogenic illness Illness that has no obvious physical cause.

Psychoneuroimmunology The study of the mind and its interaction with the immune system.

Psychosomatic illness Illness that may have a physical cause but that also has a psychological component.

Randomised controlled trial A method of experimentation in medicine whereby one group is given the drug or treatment in question and another group is not. Allocation to these groups is entirely random.

Rapid smoking A way of getting people to stop smoking by asking them to smoke continuously until they become nauseous.

Reductionism The view that all phenomena can be 'reduced' to a common denominator such as sub-atomic particles, cells, chemicals or physical processes. It is a component of the *medical model* of health and illness.

Restrained/unrestrained eating In the study of eating disorders, terms used to describe people who are either attempting to control their food intake (restrained) or those who eat what they like, when they like (unrestrained).

Rumination Ruminators are people who, when faced with stress, tend to ponder their problem without directing their thoughts at a solution.

Social readjustment rating scale An early scale to measure stress, which gives rankings of major life *stressors* ordered against each other.

Stoic acceptance A term used in the study of *coping*, especially with terminal illness and grief. Stoic acceptance is a resolution to accept what will be.

Stress inoculation training A stress-reduction technique that involves people recognising their own reactions to stress and dealing with them as a result.

Stressor Anything that causes stress.

Tension-reduction hypothesis A view that alcoholism and other addictions arise because the addictive substance has a stress-reducing value for the individual.

Theory of planned behaviour (TPB) A model of health behaviour, developed from social psychological theory, which incorporates perceived control into the prediction of behaviour, along with subjective norms and attitudes.

Type A personality A personality type associated with high levels of impatience, competitiveness and hostility. Such people are more prone to heart disease than those with a *Type B personality*.

Type B personality Defined principally by an absence of *Type A personality* characteristics.

Type C personality A personality type associated with developing cancer. Type C individuals are likely to fail to express anger openly and to 'bottle things up'.

Type I diabetes Also known as insulin-dependent diabetes. Rarer than *Type II diabetes*. Injections of insulin are necessary.

Type II diabetes Also known as non-insulin-dependent diabetes. The most common form of diabetes; injections of insulin are not necessary.

Unrestrained eating See *Restrained eating*.

Visual analogue scale A scale where people are asked to respond to a statement and do so by making a mark along a line from two extremes, such as from 'Agree totally' to 'Disagree totally'. The measure of strength of response is given by the distance the mark is made along the line.

References

Abraham, C. and Sheeran, P. (1994) Modelling and modifying young heterosexuals' HIV preventive behaviour: a review of theories, findings and educational implications. *Patient Education and Counselling* 23, 173–86.

Aikens, J.E., Kiolbasa, T.A. and Sobel, R. (1997) Psychological predictors of glycemic change with relaxation training in non-insulin-dependent diabetes mellitus. *Psychotherapy and Psychosomatics* 66, 302–6.

Ajzen, I. (1985) From intentions to action: a theory of planned behavior, in J. Kuhl and J. Beckman (eds), *Action Control: from Cognitions to Behaviors.* New York: Springer.

Ajzen, I. (1988) *Attitudes, Personality and Behavior.* Milton Keynes: Open University Press.

Ajzen, I. (1991) The theory of planned behavior. *Organizational Behavior and Human Decision Processes* 50, 179–211.

Allison, D.B., Heshka, S., Neale, M.C., Lykken, D.T. and Heymsfield, S.B. (1994) A genetic analysis of relative weight among 4,020 twin pairs, with an emphasis on sex effects. *Health Psychology* 13, 362–5.

Barber, T.X. (1982) Hypnosuggestive procedures in the treatment of clinical pain: implications for theories of hypnosis and suggestive therapy, in T. Millon, C. Green and R.B. Meagher (eds), *Handbook of Clinical Health Psychology.* New York: Plenum.

Becker, M.H., Maiman, L.A., Kirscht, J.P., Haefner, D.P. and Drachman, R.H. (1977) The health belief model and prediction of dietary compliance: a field experiment. *Journal of Health and Social Behaviour* 18, 348–66.

Beecher, H. (1946) Pain in men wounded in battle. *Bulletin of the United States Medical Department* 5, 445–54.

Beecher, H.K. (1956) Relationship of significance of wound to pain experienced. *Journal of the American Medical Association* 161, 1609–13.

Bennett, P. (2000) *Introduction to Clinical Health Psychology.* Buckingham: Open University Press.

Bennett, P. and Clatworthy, J. (1999) Smoking cessation during pregnancy: testing a psycho-biological model. *Psychology, Health & Medicine*, 4, 319–26.

Berk, L.E. (2000) *Child Development* (5th edn). Boston: Allyn & Bacon.

Berkman, L.F. and Syme, S.L. (1979) Social networks, host resistance, and mortality: a nine-year follow-up study of Alameda County residents. *American Journal of Epidemiology* 109, 186–204.

Bibace, R. and Walsh, M.E. (1979) Developmental stages in children's conceptions of illness, in G.C. Stone, F. Cohen and N.E. Adler (eds), *Health Psychology–A Handbook.* San Francisco: Jossey-Bass.

Billings, A.G. and Moos, R.H. (1981) The role of coping responses and social resources in attenuating the stress of life events. *Journal of Behavioral Medicine* 4, 139–57.

Blair, A. (1993) Social class and the contextualisation of illness experience, in A. Radley (ed.), *Worlds of Illness: Biographical and Cultural Perspectives on Health and Disease.* London: Routledge.

Blanchard, E.B. and Andrasik, F. (1985) *Management of chronic headaches: A psychological approach.* New York: Pergamon Press.

Booth, R., Koester, S., Brewster, J.T., Weibel, W.W. and Fritz, R.B. (1991) Intravenous drug users and AIDS: risk behaviors. *American Journal of Drug and Alcohol Abuse* 17, 337–53.

Bortner, R.W. (1969) A short rating scale as a potential measure of pattern A behaviour. *Journal of Chronic Disease* 22, 87–91.

Bosscher, R.J. (1993) Running and mixed physical exercise with depressed psychiatric patients. *International Journal of Sport Psychology* 24, 170–84.

Brannon, L. and Feist, J. (2000) *Health Psychology: An Introduction to Behavior and Health* (4th edn). Belman, CA: Wadsworth/Thomson Learning.

Bray, S.R., Gyurcsik, N.C., Culos-Reed, S.N., Dawson, K.A. and Martin, K.A. (2001) An exploratory investigation of the relationship between proxy efficacy, self-efficacy and exercise attendance. *Journal of Health Psychology* 6, 425–34.

Butler, C. and Steptoe, A. (1986) Placebo responses: an experimental study of psychophysiological processes in asthmatic volunteers. *British Journal of Clinical Psychology* 25, 173–83.

Cannon, W.B. (1927) The James–Lange theory of emotions: a critical examination and an alternative. *American Journal of Psychology* 39, 106–24.

Cappell, H. and Greeley, J. (1987) Alcohol and tension reduction: an update on research and theory, in H.T. Blane and K.E. Leonard (eds), *Psychological Theories of Drinking and Alcoholism*. New York: Guilford Press.

Carroll, D. and Niven, C.A. (1993) Gender, health and stress, in C. Niven and D. Carroll (eds), *The Health Psychology of Women*. Chur, Switzerland: Harwood.

Chapman, C.R., Casey, K.L., Dubner, R., Foley, K.M., Gracely, R.H. and Reading, A.E. (1985) Pain measurement: an overview. *Pain* 22, 1–31.

Charlton, A. and Blair, V. (1989) Predicting the onset of smoking in boys and girls. *Social Science and Medicine* 29, 813–18.

Cohen, S., Tyrrell, D. and Smith, A. (1993) Negative life events, perceived stress, negative affect, and susceptibility to the common cold. *Journal of Personality and Social Psychology* 64, 131–40.

Cole, A.D. and Bond, N.W. (1983) Olfactory aversion conditioning and overeating: a review and some data. *Perceptual and Motor Skills* 57, 667–78.

Conboy, J.K. (1994) The effects of exercise withdrawal on mood states in runners. *Journal of Sport Behavior* 17, 188–203.

Cooper, K.H. (1982) *The Aerobics Programme for Total Well-being*. New York: Evans.

Cooper, K.H. (1985) *Running Without Fear! How to Reduce the Risk of Heart Attacks and Sudden Death During Aerobic Exercise*. New York: Evans.

Dakof, G.A. and Taylor, S.E. (1990) Victims' perceptions of social support: what is helpful from whom? *Journal of Personality and Social Psychology* 58, 80–9.

Davis, H. and Fallowfield, L. (1994) *Counselling and Communication in Healthcare*. Chichester: John Wiley.

Derogatis, L.R., Abeloff, M.D. and Melisaratos, N. (1979) Psychological coping mechanisms and survival time in metastatic breast cancer. *Journal of the American Medical Association* 242, 1504–8.

Diego, M.A., Jones, N.A., Field, F., Hernandez-Reif, M., Schanberg, S., Kuhn, C., McAdam, V., Galamaga, R. and Galamaga, M. (1998) Aromatherapy positively affects mood, EEG patterns of alertness and math computations. *International Journal of Neuroscience* 96, 217–24.

Dowling, J. (1983) Autonomic measures and behavioural indices of pain sensitivity. *Pain* 16, 193–200.

Dunkel-Schetter, C., Feinstein, L., Taylor, S.E. and Falke, R. (1992) Patterns of coping with cancer and their correlates. *Health Psychology* 11, 79–87.

Duxbury, J. (2000) *Difficult Patients*. Oxford: Butterworth Heinemann.

Edelmann, R.J. (2000) *Psychosocial Aspects of the Health Care Process*. Harlow: Prentice Hall.

Egger, G., Fitzgerald, W., Frape, G., Monaem, A., Rubinstein, P., Tyler, C. and McKay, B. (1983) Results of large scale media antismoking campaign in Australia: North Coast 'Quit for Life' programme. *British Medical Journal* 287, 1125–8.

Eiser, C. and Twamley, S. (1999) Talking to children about health and illness, in M. Murray and K. Chamberlain (eds), *Qualitative Health Psychology*. London: Sage.

Elian, M. and Dean, G. (1985) To tell or not to tell the diagnosis of multiple sclerosis. *The Lancet* 2, 27–8.

Ellis, A. (1962) *Reason and Emotion in Psychotherapy*. New York: Lyle Stuart.

Festinger, L. (1957) *A Theory of Cognitive Dissonance*. Stanford: Stanford University Press.

Field, T., Alpert, B., Vega-Lahr, N., Goldstein, S. and Perry, S. (1988) Hospitalization stress in children: sensitizer and repressor coping styles. *Health Psychology* 7, 433–45.

File, S.E., Fluck, E. and Leahy, A. (2001) Nicotine has calming effects on stress-induced mood changes in females, but enhances aggressive mood in males. *International Journal of Neuropsychopharmacology* 4, 371–6.

Fine, P. (2000) Search for AIDS vaccine turns to brothels. *Times Higher Education Supplement*, 11 February.

Fiore, M.C., Smith, S.S., Jorenby, D.E. and Baker, T.B. (1994) The effectiveness of the nicotine patch for smoking cessation: a meta-analysis. *Journal of the American Medical Association* 271, 1940–7.

Folkman, S., Lazarus, R.S., Dunkel-Schetter, C., DeLongis, A. and Gruen, R.J. (1986) Dynamics of a stressful encounter: cognitive appraisal, coping, and encounter outcomes. *Journal of Personality and Social Psychology* 50, 992–1003.

Forshaw, M. (2002a) Dyslexic patients: emerging issues. *Health Psychology Update* 11, 54–5.

Forshaw, M. (2002b) *Essential Health Psychology*. London: Arnold.

Foster, G.D., Wadden, T.A., Kendall, P.C., Stunkard, A.J. and Vogt, R.A. (1996) Psychological effects of weight loss and regain: a prospective study. *Journal of Consulting and Clinical Psychology* 64, 752–7.

Frankenhaeuser, M. (1975) Sympathetic adrenomedullary activity behavior and the psychosocial environment, in P.H. Venables and M.J. Christie (eds), *Research in Psychophysiology*. New York: Wiley.

French, A.P. and Tupin, J.P. (1974) Therapeutic application of a simple relaxation method. *American Journal of Psychotherapy* 28, 282–7.

Freudenberger, H.J. (1974) Staff burn-out. *Journal of Social Issues* 30, 159–65.

Friedman, M. and Rosenman, R.H. (1959) Association of specific overt behaviour pattern with blood and cardiovascular findings. *Journal of the American Medical Association* 169, 1286–97.

Friedman, M. and Rosenman, R.H. (1974) *Type A Behavior and Your Heart*. New York: Knopf.

Gale, E.A.M. and Anderson, J.V. (1998) Diabetes mellitus and other disorders of metabolism, in Kumar, P. and Clark, M. (eds), *Clinical Medicine* (4th edn). Edinburgh: W.B. Saunders.

Garner, D.M. and Wooley, S.C. (1991) Confronting the failure of behavioral and dietary treatments for obesity. *Clinical Psychology Review* 11, 729–80.

Gatchel, R.J., Baum, A. and Krantz, D.S. (1989) *An Introduction to Health Psychology* (2nd edn). New York: Random House.

General Household Survey (1999) London: Office of Population Censuses and Surveys.

Glasser, R.J. (1976) *The Body is the Hero*. New York: Random House.

Goldstein, K. (1939) *The organism*. New York: American Book Co. (Van Nostrand).

Goolkasian, P. (1985) Phase and sex effects in pain perception: a critical review. *Psychology of Women Quarterly* 9, 15–28.

Gourlay, S.G., Forbes, A., Marriner, T., Pethica, D. and McNeil, J.J. (1994) Prospective study of factors predicting outcome of transdermal nicotine treatment in smoking cessation. *British Medical Journal* 309, 842–6.

Graham, H. (1998) Health at risk: poverty and national health strategies, in Doyal, L. (ed.), *Women and Health Services*. Buckingham: Open University Press.

Greer, S. (1991) Psychological response to cancer and survival. *Psychological Medicine* 21, 40–9.

Gruzelier, J., Levy, J., Williams, J. and Henderson, D. (2001) Self-hypnosis and exam stress: comparing immune and relaxation-related imagery for influences on immunity, health, and mood. *Contemporary Hypnosis* 18, 73–86.

Hadlow, J. and Pitts, M. (1991) The understanding of common health terms by doctors, nurses and patients. *Social Science and Medicine* 32, 193–6.

Hall, J.A., Irish, J.T., Roter, D.L., Ehrlich, C.M. and Miller, L.H. (1994) Gender in medical encounters: an analysis of physician and patient communication in a primary care setting. *Health Psychology*, 13, 384–92.

Hamburg, B.A. and Inoff, G.E. (1982) Relationship between behavioral factors and diabetic control in children and adolescents: a camp study. *Psychosomatic Medicine* 44, 321–9.

Hampson, S.E. (1997) Illness representations and the self-management of diabetes, in K.J. Petrie and J.A. Weinman (eds), *Perceptions of Health & Illness*. Amsterdam: Harwood Academic.

Herman, C.P. and Mack, D. (1975) Restrained and unrestrained eating. *Journal of Personality* 43, 647–60.

Heusinkveld, K.B. (1997) Cancer prevention and risk assessment. In C. Varricchio, M. Pierce, C. Walker and T.B. Ades (eds), *A cancer source book for nurses* (7th ed.) (pp.35–42). Atlanta: The American Cancer Society.

Hogbin, B. and Fallowfield, L.J. (1989) Getting it taped: the 'bad news' consultation with cancer patients. *British Journal of Hospital Medicine* 41, 330–3.

Holmes, D.S. (1984) Meditation and somatic arousal reduction: a review of the experimental evidence. *American Psychologist* 39, 1–10.

Holmes, T.H. and Rahe, R.H. (1967) The social readjustment rating scale. *Journal of Psychosomatic Research* 11, 213–18.

Houston, W.R. (1995) Personality traits of morbidly obese women seeking gastroplasty surgery. *Dissertation Abstracts International Section B: Sciences and Engineering* 56, 1733.

Houtsmuller, E.J. and Stitzer, M.L. (1999) Manipulation of cigarette craving through rapid smoking: efficacy and effects on smoking behavior. *Psychopharmacology* 142, 149–57.

Jackson, C. and Lindsay, S. (1995) Reducing anxiety in new dental patients by means of a leaflet. *British Dental Journal* 179, 163–7.

Jacobsen, P.B., Bovbjerg, D.H. and Redd, W.H. (1993) Anticipatory anxiety in patients receiving cancer chemotherapy. *Health Psychology* 12, 469–75.

Jensen, M.P. and Karoly, P. (1991) Motivation and expectancy factors in symptom perception: a laboratory study of the placebo effect. *Psychosomatic Medicine* 53, 144–52.

Jessor, R. and Jessor, S.L. (1977) *Problem Behavior and Psychosocial Development: A Longitudinal Study of Youth*. New York: Academic Press.

Johnston, D.W., Cook, D.G. and Shaper, A.G. (1987) Type A behaviour and ischaemic heart disease in middle aged British men. *British Medical Journal* 295, 86–9.

Kanner, A.D., Coyne, I.C., Schaefer, C. and Lazarus, R.S. (1981) Comparison of two modes of stress measurement: daily hassles and uplifts versus major life events. *Journal of Behavioral Medicine* 4, 1–39.

Kelleher, D. (1988) Coming to terms with diabetes: coping strategies and non-compliance, in R. Anderson and M. Bury (eds), *Living with Chronic Illness*, London: Allen & Unwin.

Kent, G. and Dalgleish, M. (1996) *Psychology and Medical Care* (3rd edn). London: W.B. Saunders.

Kessler, R.C., Kendler, K.S., Heath, A.C., Neale, M.C. and Eaves, L.J. (1992) Social support, depressed mood, and adjustment to stress: a genetic epidemiological investigation. *Journal of Personality and Social Psychology* 62, 257–72.

Kiernan, P.J. and Isaacs, J.B. (1981) Use of drugs by the elderly. *Journal of the Royal Society of Medicine* 74, 196–200.

Killen, J.D., Robinson, T.N., Haydel, K.F., Hayward, C., Wilson, D.M., Hammer, L.D., Litt, I.F. and Taylor, C.B. (1997) Prospective study of risk factors for the initiation of cigarette smoking. *Journal of Consulting and Clinical Psychology* 65, 1011–16.

King, A.C., Oman, R.F., Brassington, G.S., Bliwise, D.L. and Haskell, W.L. (1997) Moderate-intensity exercise and self-rated quality of sleep in older adults: A randomized controlled trial. *Journal of the American Medical Association* 277, 32–7.

Kobasa, S.C. (1979) Stressful life events, personality, and health: an inquiry into hardiness. *Journal of Personality and Social Psychology* 37, 1–11.

Korsch, B.M. and Negrete, V. (1972) Doctor–patient communication. *Scientific American* 227, 66–74.

Krantz, D.S., Durel, L.A., Davia, J.E., Shaffer, R.T., Arabian, J.M., Dembroski, T.M. and MacDougall, J.N. (1982) Propranolol medication among coronary patients: relationship to Type A behavior and cardiovascular response. *Journal of Human Stress* 8, 4–12.

Kuhn, M.A. (1999) *Complementary Therapies for Health Care Providers*. Philadelphia: Lippincott Williams & Wilkins.

Lando, H.A. (1977) Successful treatment of smokers with a broad-spectrum behavioral approach. *Journal of Consulting and Clinical Psychology* 45, 361–6.

Langewitz, W., Wossmer, B., Iseli, J. and Berger, W. (1997) Psychological and metabolic improvement after an outpatient teaching program for functional intensified insulin therapy. *Diabetes Research and Clinical Practice* 37, 157–64.

Lazarus, R. (1966) *Psychological Stress and the Coping Process.* New York: McGraw-Hill.

Leventhal, H. and Avis, N. (1976) Pleasure, addiction, and habit: factors in verbal report or factors in smoking behavior? *Journal of Abnormal Psychology* 85, 478–88.

Leventhal, H. and Cleary, P.D. (1980) The smoking problem: a review of research and theory in behavioral risk modification. *Psychological Bulletin* 88, 370–405.

Leventhal, H., Easterling, D.V., Coons, H., Luchterhand, C. and Love, R.R. (1986) Adaptation to chemotherapy treatments, in B. Anderson (ed.), *Women with Cancer.* New York: Springer Verlag.

Lewis, C.E., Rachelefsky, G., Lewis, M.A., de la Sota, A. and Kaplan, M. (1984) A randomised trial of ACT (asthma care training) for kids. *Pediatrics* 74, 478–86.

Ley, P. (1989) Improving patients' understanding, recall, satisfaction and compliance, in A.K. Broome (ed.) *Health Psychology.* London: Chapman & Hall.

Ley, P. (1997) Compliance among patients, in A. Baum, S. Newman, J. Weinman, R. West and C. McManus (eds), *Cambridge Handbook of Psychology, Health and Medicine.* Cambridge: Cambridge University Press.

Lifson, A., Hessol, N., Rutherford, G.W. *et al.* (1989) The Natural History of HIV Infection in a Cohort of Homosexual and Bisexual men: Clinical manifestations, 1978–1989. In the Vth International Conference on AIDS, Montreal, September.

Litt, M.D., Kadden, R.M., Cooney, N.L. and Kabela, E. (2003) Coping skills and treatment outcomes in cognitive-behavioral and interactional group therapy for alcoholism. *Journal of Consulting and Clinical Psychology* 71, 118–28.

Longabaugh, R. and Morgenstern, J. (1999) Cognitive-behavioral coping-skills therapy for alcohol dependence: current status and future directions. *Alcohol Research and Health* 23, 78–85.

Luria, A.R. (1958) *The Mind of a Mnemonist.* New York: Basic Books.

Marks, G., Richardson, J.L. and Maldonado, N. (1991) Self disclosure of HIV infection to sexual partners. *American Journal of Public Health* 81, 1321–3.

Marshall, J.R. and Funch, D.P. (1986) Gender and illness behaviour among colorectal cancer patients. *Women and Health* 11, 67–82.

Martinsen, E.W. and Morgan, W.P. (1997) Antidepressant effects of physical activity, in W.P. Morgan (ed.), *Physical Activity and Mental Health.* Washington: Taylor & Francis.

Maslach, C. (1982) *Burnout: The Cost of Caring.* New York: Prentice Hall.

Maslow, A.H. (1962) *Toward a Psychology of Being.* Princeton, NJ: Van Nostrand.

Mays, V.M. and Cochran, S.D. (1988) Issues in the perception of AIDS risk and risk reduction activities by black and Hispanic/Latina women. *American Psychologist* 43, 949–57.

Mazzulo, J.M., Lasagna, L. and Griner, P. (1974) Variation in interpretation of prescription instructions. *Journal of the American Medical Association* 227, 29–31.

McAuley, E. (1993) Self-efficacy and the maintenance of exercise participation in older adults. *Journal of Behavioral Medicine* 16, 103–13.

McAvoy, B.R. and Raza, R. (1988) Asian women: (i) contraceptive knowledge, attitudes and usage; (ii) contraceptive services and cervical cytology. *Health Trends* 20, 11–17.

Mechanic, D. (1978) *Medical Sociology* (2nd edn). New York: Free Press.

Meichenbaum, D. and Deffenbacher, J.L. (1988) Stress inoculation training. *Counseling Psychologist* 16, 69–90.

Melzack, R. (1975) The McGill Pain Questionnaire: major properties and scoring methods. *Pain* 1, 277–99.

Melzack, R. and Wall, P. (1965) Pain mechanisms: a new theory. *Science* 150, 971–9.

Melzack, R. and Wall, P. (1982) *The Challenge of Pain.* Harmondsworth: Penguin.

Merikle, P.M. and Skanes, H.E. (1992) Subliminal self-help audiotapes: a search for placebo effects. *Journal of Applied Psychology,* 77, 772–6.

Miller, C.T. and Downey, K.T. (1999) A meta-analysis of heavyweight and self-esteem. *Journal of Consulting and Clinical Psychology* 65, 448–52.

References

Miller, T.Q., Smith, T.W., Turner C.W., Guijarro, M.L. and Hallet, A.J. (1996) A meta-analytic review of research on hostility and physical health. *Psychological Bulletin* 119, 322–48.

Montgomery, J. (1997) *Health Care Law*. Oxford: Oxford University Press.

Mosbach, P. and Leventhal, H. (1988) Peer group identification and smoking: implications for intervention. *Journal of Abnormal Psychology* 97, 238–45.

Napoleon, H. (1999) *Yuuyaraq*: the way of the human being, in C. Samson (ed.), *Health Studies: A Critical and Cross-Cultural Reader*. Oxford: Blackwell.

Newton, J. (1995) The readability and utility of general dental practice patient information leaflets: an evaluation. *British Dental Journal* 178, 329–32.

Nichols, K.A. (1993) *Psychological Care in Physical Illness* (2nd edn). London: Chapman & Hall.

Nolen-Hoeksema, S., McBride, A. and Larson, J. (1997) Rumination and psychological distress among bereaved partners. *Journal of Personality and Social Psychology* 72, 855–62.

O'Connor, P.J. (1997) Overtraining and staleness, in W.P. Morgan (ed.), *Physical Activity and Mental Health*. Washington: Taylor & Francis.

Oakeshott, P., Kerry, S., Hay, S. and Hay, P. (2000) Condom promotion in women attending inner city general practices for cervical smears: a randomised controlled trial. *Family Practice* 17, 56–9.

Oakley, A. (1980) *Women Confined*. Oxford: Martin Robertson.

Office of National Statistics (1999) *Social Trends* 29, London: The Stationery Office.

Ogden, J. (2000) *Health Psychology: A Textbook* (2nd end). Buckingham: Open University Press.

Pennington, D. (ed.) (2002) *Introducing Psychology: Approaches, Topics and Methods*. London: Hodder & Stoughton.

Pennington, D., Smithson, R., McLoughlin, J., Robinson, D. and Boswell, K. (2003) *Advanced Psychology: Child Development, Perspectives and Methods*. London: Hodder & Stoughton.

Pettingale, K.W., Morris, T., Greer, S. and Haybittle, J.L. (1985) Mental attitudes to cancer: an additional prognostic factor. *The Lancet* 1, 750.

Pomerleau, O.F. and Pomerleau, C.S. (1989) A biobehavioral perspective on smoking, in T. Ney and A. Gale (eds), *Smoking and Behavior*. Chichester: John Wiley.

Porter, R. (1997) *The Greatest Benefit to Mankind: A Medical History of Humanity From Antiquity to the Present*. London: HarperCollins.

Povey, R., Conner, M., Sparks, P., James, R. and Shepherd, R. (2000) Application of the theory of planned behaviour to two dietary behaviours: roles of perceived control and self-efficacy. *British Journal of Health Psychology* 5, 121–39.

Raglin, J.S. (1997) Anxiolytic effects of physical activity. In W.P. Morgan (ed.), *Physical activity and mental health* (pp.107–26). Washington, DC: Taylor & Francis.

Reed, G.M., Kemeny, M.E., Taylor, S.E. and Visscher, B.R. (1999) Negative HIV-specific expectancies and AIDS-related bereavement as predictors of symptom onset in asymptomatic HIV-positive gay men. *Health Psychology* 18, 354–63.

Rigby, K., Brown, M., Anganostou, P., Ross, M.W. *et al.* (1989) Shock tactics to counter AIDS: the Australian experience. *Psychology and Health* 3, 145–59.

Rosenstock, I.M. (1966) Why people use health services. *Millbank Memorial Fund Quarterly* 44, 94–124.

Roth, S. and Cohen, L.J. (1986) Approach, avoidance, and coping with stress. *American Psychologist* 41, 813–19.

Rotter, J.B. (1966) Generalized expectancies for internal versus external control of reinforcement. *Psychological Monographs* 80(1) (Whole No. 609).

Salmon, P. (2000) *Psychology of Medicine and Surgery*. Chichester: John Wiley.

Salovey, P. and Birnbaum, D. (1989) Influence of mood on health-relevant cognitions. *Journal of Personality and Social Psychology* 57, 539–51.

Sarafino, E.P. (1994) *Health Psychology: Biopsychosocial Interactions* (2nd edn). Oxford: Wiley.

Sarafino, E.P. (2002) *Health Psychology: Biopsychosocial Interactions* (4th edn). New York: Wiley.

Savage, R. and Armstrong, D. (1990) Effect of a general practitioner's consulting style on patient satisfaction: a controlled study. *British Medical Journal* 301, 968–70.

Schachter, S. (1977) Nicotine regulation in heavy and light smokers. *Journal of Experimental Psychology: General* 106, 5–12.

Schifter, D.E. and Ajzen, I. (1985) Intention, perceived control, and weight loss: an application of the theory of planned behavior. *Journal of Personality and Social Psychology* 49, 843–51.

Schmidt, W. (1977) Cirrhosis and alcohol consumption: an epidemiological perspective, in G. Edwards and M. Grant (eds), *Alcoholism: New Knowledge and New Responses*. London: Croom Helm.

Schwarzer, R. (1992) Self-efficacy in the adoption and maintenance of health behaviors: Theoretical approaches and a new model, in R. Schwarzer (ed.), *Self-Efficacy: Thought Control of Action*. Washington, DC: Hemisphere.

Seidell, J.C and Rissenen, A.M. (1998) Time trends in world-wide prevalence of obesity, in G.A. Bray, C. Bouchard and W.P.T James (eds), *Handbook of Obesity*. New York: Marcel Dekker.

Shaffer, J.W., Graves, P.L., Swank, R.T. and Pearson, T.A. (1987) Clustering of personality traits in youth and the subsequent development of cancer in physicians. *Journal of Behavioral Medicine* 10, 441–7.

Sheeran, P. and Abraham, C. (1995) The health belief model, in M. Conner and P. Norman (eds), *Predicting Health Behaviour*. Buckingham: Open University Press.

Shekelle, R.B., Rossof, A.H. and Stamler, J. (1991) Dietary cholesterol and incidence of lung cancer: the Western Electric study. *Journal of Epidemiology* 134, 480–4.

Shiffman, S., Paty, J.A., Gnys, M., Kassel, J.D. and Elash, C. (1995) Nicotine withdrawal in chippers and regular smokers: subjective and cognitive effects. *Health Psychology* 14, 301–9.

Shontz, F.C. (1975) *The Psychological Aspects of Physical Disease and Disability*. New York: Macmillan.

Siegel, K., Schrimshaw, E.W. and Dean, L. (1999) Symptom Interpretation and medication adherence among late middle-age and older HIV-infected adults. *Journal of Health Psychology* 4, 247–57.

Simonton, O.C. and Simonton, S.S. (1975) Belief systems and the management of emotional aspects of malignancy. *Journal of Transpersonal Psychology* 7, 29–47.

Sinyor, D., Schwartz, J.G., Peronnet, F., Bisson, G. and Seraganian, P. (1983) Aerobic fitness level and reactivity to psychosocial stress. *Psychosomatic Medicine* 45, 205–17.

Slattery, M.L., Boucher, K.M., Caan, B.J., Potter, J.D. and Ma, K.N. (1998) Eating patterns and risk of colon cancer. *American Journal of Epidemiology* 148, 4–16.

Slay, H.A., Hayaki, J., Napolitano, M.A. and Brownell, K.D. (1998) Motivation for running and eating attitudes in obligatory versus non-obligatory runners. *International Journal of Eating Disorders* 23, 267–75.

Sonstroem, R.J. (1997) Physical activity and self-esteem, in W.P. Morgan (ed.), *Physical Activity and Mental Health*. Washington: Taylor & Francis.

Sosa, R., Kennell, J., Klaus, M., Robertson, S. and Urrutia, J. (1980) The effect of a supportive companion on perinatal problems, length of labor and mother–infant interaction. *New England Journal of Medicine* 303, 597–600.

Spiegel, D. and Moore, R. (1997) Imagery and hypnosis in the treatment of cancer patients. *Oncology* 11, 1179–89.

Spitzer, L. and Rodin, J. (1981) Human eating behaviour: a critical review of studies in normal weight and overweight individuals. *Appetite* 2, 293–329.

Stall, R.D., Coates, T.J. and Hoff, C. (1988) Behavioral risk reduction for HIV infection among gay and bisexual men: a review of results from the United States. *American Psychologist* 43, 878–85.

Stampfer, M.J., Hennekens, C.H., Manson, J.E., Colditz, G.A., Rosner, D. and Willett, W.C. (1993) Vitamin E consumption and the risk of coronary heart disease in women. *New England Journal of Medicine* 328, 1444–9.

Stein, P.N. and Motta, R.W. (1992) Effects of aerobic and nonaerobic exercise on depression and self-esteem. *Perceptual and Motor Skills* 74, 79–89.

Stein, Z.A. (1990) HIV prevention: the need for methods women can use. *American Journal of Public Health* 80, 460–2.

Stroebe, W. (2000) *Social Psychology and Health* (2nd edn). Buckingham: Open University Press.

Suls, J. and Fletcher, B. (1985) The relative efficacy of avoidant and non-avoidant coping strategies: a meta-analysis. *Health Psychology* 4, 249–88.

Tattersall, M.H., Butow, P.N., Griffin, A.-M. and Dunn, S.M. (1994) The take-home message: patients prefer consultation audiotapes to summary letters. *Journal of Clinical Oncology* 12, 1305–11.

Taylor, N.M., Hall, G.M. and Salmon, P. (1996) Patients' experiences of patient-controlled analgesia. *Anaesthesia* 51, 525–8.

Taylor, S.E., Lichtman, R.R. and Wood, J.V. (1984) Attributions, beliefs about control, and adjustment to breast cancer. *Journal of Personality and Social Psychology* 46, 489–502.

Tedesco, L.A., Keffer, M.A. and Fleck-Kandath, C. (1991) Self-efficacy, reasoned action and oral behavior reports: A social cognitive approach to compliance. *Journal of Behavior Medicine* 14, 341–55.

Temoshok, L. (1987) Personality, coping style, emotion and cancer: toward an integrative model. *Social Science and Medicine* 20, 833–40.

Temoshok. L., Sweet, D.M. and Zich, J.A. (1987) A three city comparison of the public's knowledge and attitudes about AIDS. *Psychology and Health* 1, 43–60.

Totman, R.G. (1987) *The Social Causes of Illness.* London: Souvenir Press.

Toynbee, P. (1977) *Patients.* New York: Harcourt Brace.

Trevisan, M., Krogh, V., Freudenheim, J., Blake, A., Muti, P., Panico, S., Farinaro, E., Mancini, M., Menotti, A. and Ricci, G. (1990) Consumption of olive oil, butter, and vegetable oils and coronary heart disease risk factors. *Journal of the American Medical Association* 263, 688–92.

Turk, D.C., Rudy, T.E. and Sorkin, B.A. (1992) Chronic pain: Behavioural conceptualizations and interventions. In S.M. Turner, K.S. Calhoun and H.E. Adams (eds), *Handbook of clinical behaviour therapy* (2nd ed). New York: Wiley.

US Department of Health, Education, and Welfare and US Public Health Service, Centers for Disease Control and Prevention (1964) *Smoking and Health: Report of the Advisory Committee to the Surgeon General of the Public Health Service (Publication No. PHS-1103).* Washington, DC: US Government Printing Office.

Wadden, T.A. and Anderton, C.H. (1982) The clinical use of hypnosis. *Psychological Bulletin* 91, 215–43.

Waldron, E. (1976) Why do women live longer than men? *Journal of Human Stress* 2, 2–13.

Walker, L.S., Garber, J. and Greene, J.W. (1991) Somatization symptoms in pediatric abdominal pain patients: relation to chronicity of abdominal pain and parent somatization. *Journal of Abnormal Child Psychology* 19, 379–94.

Walton, K.G., Pugh, N.D., Gelderloos, P. and Macrae, P. (1995) Stress reduction and preventing hypertension: preliminary support for a psychoneuroendocrine mechanism. *Journal of Alternative and Complementary Medicine* 1, 263–83.

Wardle, J. and Beales, S. (1988) Control and loss of control over eating: an experimental investigation. *Journal of Abnormal Psychology* 97, 35–40.

Wiens, A.N. and Menustik, C.E. (1983) Treatment outcome and patient characteristics in an aversion therapy program for alcoholism. *American Psychologist* 38, 1089–96.

Wilkinson, S. (1991) Factors which influence how nurses communicate with cancer patients. *Journal of Advanced Nursing* 16, 677–88.

Wolpe. J. (1958) *Psychotherapy by Reciprocal Inhibition.* Stanford: Stanford University Press.

Yong, L.C., Brown, C.C., Schatzkin, A., Dresser, C.M. *et al.* (1997) Intake of vitamins E, C and A, and risk of lung cancer. *American Journal of Epidemiology* 146, 231–43.

Index